{Simply Unexpected}

Stories of a Down syndrome birth diagnosis

As told by families around the world

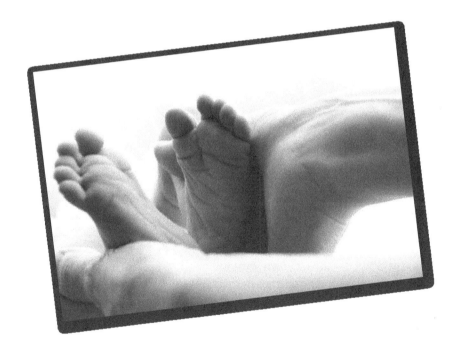

Compiled by Jennifer Jacob and Joelle Kelly

www.missiont21.com

This book is not intended as a substitute for the medical advice of physicians. The reader should regularly consult a physician in matters relating to his/her health and particularly with respect to any symptoms that may require diagnosis or medical attention. These stories are written by parents of children with Down syndrome. This book is not written as a medical reference, it is written as a reflection of memories from the diagnosis time from parents' perspectives.

Although the authors and publisher have made every effort to ensure that the information in this book was correct at press time, the author and publisher do not assume and hereby disclaim any liability to any party for any loss, damage, or disruption caused by errors or omissions, whether such errors or omissions result from negligence, accident, or any other cause.

Because families from around the world contributed to this work, spelling, phrases and language were kept in the context of the geographic location.

ISBN 978-1-312-26867-8

Visit our website @ http://www.missiont21.com/

Made available through support and funding by Down Syndrome Diagnosis Network (DSDN)
http://www.dsdiagnosisnetwork.org/

{Simply Unexpected}

{Appreciation}

This book really is a true work of heart. So many mothers and fathers poured their hearts into these stories so that other families might feel a bit less alone in this journey. None of us expected to be on this adventure, but as you read, you realize how life-changing it has been for many families. Our greatest hope is that you see bits of yourself and your story here and that you will feel the tremendous sense of community, family and support that is the world of Down syndrome.

We are so grateful to all the moms and dads that were honest, vulnerable and sincere in what their diagnosis story was. As you authored your story, your genuine selves were shown. It was fantastic therapy session for many of us and uncovered much learning and understanding.

Many thanks to the many moms who shared their talents in editing, marketing, artistry, publishing and creativity to help this novice team pull together a great work; sharing your talents has made all the difference in this project. From all over the world we came together for a common focus and what a result!

Most of us never imagined that our lives stories would become intertwined together. To all the women around the world that we now count as friends and family, THANK YOU. What a difference this will make in the lives of families for years to come.

~ Jen and Joelle

{Welcome to the family}

Odds are that if you are choosing this book, you or a loved one has entered into the world of Trisomy 21 (T21), also known as Down syndrome, probably with little warning or preparation.

It is also highly likely that you may be scared, confused, anxious, or even terrified. Often those feelings are al so accompanied by deep love and concern for your new or unborn baby. It is quite a paradox and can really send you into a tailspin. You love your child so much, yet all your background knowledge (which for many of us was very limited) and inner voice may scream out, "This is the worst news possible!"

Breathe.
Stop Googling.
Breathe again.

We have been there. And we want to tell you this: it really gets better. *Really.*
Not long ago we were in your shoes and feeling exactly the same things.
Through our stories, you will see bits of yourself. You will see pieces of your family. You will see your new baby and, potentially, his or her future.

You will see that life does not come crashing down and that your child will fold into your family like any other baby. Well, maybe not like any other baby. You may notice the intense stare as your baby seems to look into your heart and soul.

Our purpose in writing this book is to add to the resources for new and expecting parents with a T21 diagnosis. We want to share our experiences and stories and provide a realistic view of what it means to welcome a baby into your family with Down syndrome. Our hope is that, through our words and photographs, you are able to glimpse into the future and more easily accept your baby and all that may come and see that it truly is a blessing, like any other child.

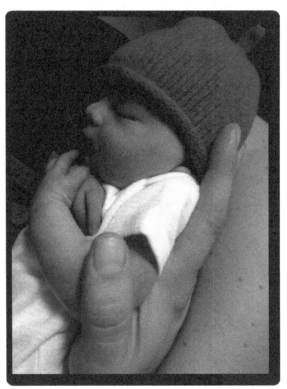

{Simply Unexpected}

Receiving a Birth Diagnosis

The birth of a child typically evokes feelings of joy, excitement, and celebration. But for many women whose babies receive a birth diagnosis of Down syndrome, the emotions can be decidedly different: sadness, confusion, fear. There is no right or wrong reaction, but many families have eerily similar accounts of those seemingly dark first days.

The baby you have prepared for so diligently is not at all what you expected. You may feel bewildered. You may have feelings of grief, confusion, and worry, yet your love for that baby—YOUR baby—is incredibly real and as strong as any bond between a parent and child.

At first, every second is filled with new thoughts, feelings, and fears. The unknown future and your lack of preparation now top your list of worries. What will your baby's life be like as they grow up? How will you handle the increased responsibility that comes with having child with special needs? And perhaps most poignant, how will the arrival of this baby, with its unexpected extra needs, affect your other children?

But those first confusing, terrifying seconds turn to minutes, then to hours, and finally to days and months passing with your baby. You are smiling again. Your baby is smiling, cooing and snuggling, and bonding with your other children—and they with him. You realize that your baby is just that: a baby, more alike than different in so many beautiful ways.

Down syndrome is now a part of your life, but it has not become your life.

{Our Stories}

{Darcy}

So many people tell you to trust your instincts; your gut feeling that says something isn't quite right. Throughout my second pregnancy I had a feeling of uneasiness that I simply couldn't explain. I made every attempt to shrug off this feeling and believe all was well, but in the depths of my existence I knew it wasn't, I just didn't know why or how. It was day two of Darcy's life when I understood for the first time, what that gut instinct was trying to tell me.

Darcy was born 5 weeks prematurely by emergency caesarean on 21st November 2010. When my obstetrician held up our beautiful little boy in the theatre for us to see for the first time I remember thinking how perfect he looked. He weighed 5lb 8oz and was chubbier and healthier than his older brother Charlie who was born 6 weeks early and weighed just 4lb 3oz. Mark and I held him for a short moment before he was taken to the special care nursery for assistance with breathing. My husband went with Darcy to the Special Care Unit (SCU). After a short time, he proudly came to my room and told me what a good looking little man we had. Later in the day, I was able to go into the special care unit and I marvelled at how perfect our little boy was. As I put my hands into the humidicrib and touched him, putting my finger into his tiny little hand, I was overcome with love for our little bundle. I spent the first night of Darcy's life as a loving new mother, proudly telling everyone that our second beautiful son had been born and was doing very well. Our family was complete and the world seemed perfect.

The following day, my perfect world turned utterly and completely upside down. Mark had gone to work and I had a friend visiting when a nurse came to tell me the paediatrician wanted to talk to me about Darcy. I eagerly headed off to the SCU expecting to hear news of how well he was doing and how he was easily breathing on his own. What was waiting for me was something life changing, something I never expected in a million years. In a gentle but assertive voice, our paediatrician said the words a mother never wants to hear…"We think your baby has Down syndrome." I will remember those words for the rest of my life as clearly as if they had just been spoken and my spine still tingles when I think about it.

In that moment, the world around me stood absolutely still and I felt so alone. I remember feeling a cold chill take over my body. My stomach wretched as if I was about to throw up and my ears were ringing. My legs shook and the floor beneath me felt as though it was going to collapse. The doctor proceeded to show me the line across Darcy's palm, the extra skin in the corners of his eyes, the slightly upward slant of his eyes. I could hear her talking but I did not comprehend a thing she was saying. Big, warm tears poured down my face and began dropping onto my beautiful little boy. The only words I managed were, "Are you sure?" A blood test would be done, but she was 90% sure. 90% I thought to myself. That meant she wasn't certain and there was still a chance she was wrong.

The hardest phone call I have ever made in my life was to tell Mark. To this day I am not sure how I got the words out of my mouth but I managed to say, "The doctor thinks Darcy has Down syndrome". Mark came straight to the hospital and again our paediatrician went through the physical signs. We listened but could barely speak. After a short time we went back to my room and fell into each other's arms, sobbing uncontrollably.

We wanted to believe the doctors and nurses were wrong. There had been no indicators during our pregnancy to suggest our baby had anything wrong with him and we couldn't understand how the medical fraternity could let us down so badly by missing this diagnosis. We hoped and prayed that there might be a miracle, but in our heart and soul we knew our Darcy had Down syndrome. 24 hours later, our paediatrician confirmed the diagnosis of Trisomy 21. Mark and I cried more than a river of tears in the following few days. We grieved openly and honestly together. Initially, it seemed as though the emotional attachment we had to Darcy when he was first born had disappeared and we felt completely detached, like he wasn't really ours. We felt cheated out of the chance to have a "normal" child and we had fleeting moments when we thought we didn't want this baby.

The first time I saw Charlie after Darcy's diagnosis, I hugged him tighter than I ever had before. Suddenly, my cheeky, naughty little toddler seemed so perfect and I felt the need to keep him very close to me in a selfish attempt to help ease the terrible pain I was feeling. Ironically, while Charlie was the one thing that helped me to smile at that time, he was also foremost in my mind as the tears flowed—I couldn't bear to think about the impact it would have on him to have a brother with Down syndrome. He didn't ask for a brother with a disability and it was so incredibly unfair to impose it upon him in his life.

The emotions we felt at this time were so strong and so overwhelming that I couldn't imagine ever feeling like I could cope with this news. These feelings lasted for what seemed like an eternity. In reality it was only a few days before we realised that our little man didn't ask to be born with Down syndrome and what he needed more than anything in the world was parents who would love him unconditionally. We came to a place of acceptance and from that point forward, we have loved our little boy with every ounce of our being.

Darcy was in the special care unit of the hospital for two weeks. In that time he was poked and prodded more than any poor little baby should ever have to experience. Initially the paediatrician believed that Darcy's heart was fine. Mark and I were very relieved about this, since we had been told that heart problems were very common for children with Down syndrome. The greatest immediate concern was Darcy's bilirubin levels and he spent quite a lot of time under lights to try to improve his jaundice. Every day the staff from pathology came to take his blood to see if his bilirubin levels were improving; and every day they were amazed at just how well he handled all the testing. Even at such a young age, Darcy's bravery and resilience were clearly evident and we have seen him demonstrate these characteristics many times in his short life.

Each day Darcy's paediatrician conducted a thorough review of his heath. During one of these checks, when Darcy was just five days old, she located a "non-innocent murmur" in his heart that she was concerned about. We were immediately referred to a paediatric cardiologist for further investigation. I can clearly remember that this was the moment when my very strong protective maternal instinct kicked in and I felt a sudden urge to do everything I could to make sure our little boy was going to be alright. Only days before we had wondered whether we really wanted this child in our lives. Now we were placed in a situation where there could be something seriously wrong with our baby and in an instant I transitioned from a grieving, uncertain mother, to a mother who fiercely wanted to nurture and shield my baby from harm. I was panicked and terrified and frightened and oh so protective. I held my little boy close to me as often as the special care nurses would allow in the hope that he would feel my strength and know I was fighting for him. Two days later Darcy had tests conducted on his heart and the specialist diagnosed thickening of the pulmonary valve. It was not immediately life threatening and the cardiologist was happy to review him in two months.

While in hospital, Darcy had two hearing tests conducted as his left ear did not pass. We were referred to have more tests done after being discharged. He also had an ultrasound done on his kidneys as pre-natal testing identified that his kidneys were enlarged. This also needed to be reviewed again in a couple of months. Thankfully, none of these health issues were major and we were discharged from the hospital with a list of things that needed to be reviewed, but nothing urgent or life threatening. By the time we were able to take Darcy home, I was an expert on medical terms related to his health. I educated myself so I could understand everything that needed to be watched or monitored. I recall during one of Darcy's hospital stays later in his life, some paediatric medical students were asking questions about his history. I rattled off everything Darcy had been through and one of them asked me if I was a nurse. I chuckled and said I was just a "Well educated Mummy"!

Following Darcy's release from hospital at two weeks of age, we did the best we could to "normalise" our family life. We really were at a place of acceptance and we had gone past the stage of grieving and were instead sponges for information about what the Down syndrome diagnosis meant for our little boy. We read many books, some encouraging and others that were confronting and difficult to comprehend. One such book that we found particularly hard to read outlined all the possible health problems a child with Down syndrome could have in their life. The list went on and on and on and as I read, a sense of panic and fear washed over me again. Eventually I put the book away for later reference, in case we ever needed it, secretly hoping we would never have to refer to it again.

Darcy was five weeks old when the most significant of his health problems became apparent. It was Christmas Eve 2010. We were all excited about the celebrations that were planned for the following day. Like every other day we bathed Darcy in the evening and I placed him on the change table to dress him. As he looked up at me, I saw for the first time cloudy cataracts in both his eyes. I knew instantly they were cataracts. That awful dreaded book I had been reading said that cataracts were a possible health concern for people with Down syndrome and I was certain that was what I was seeing. In an instant my whole world crumbled again and I felt that same sinking, wretching feeling that came over me when Darcy was first diagnosed. I had come to terms with having a child with Down syndrome. I had been reading about ways to help Darcy learn through visual and sensory stimulation. How was I going to cope with a child who had Down syndrome and was also blind?

Being Christmas, there were no specialists available and we had to wait over a week before we could finally see an ophthalmologist. We were immediately referred to see a paediatric ophthalmologist in Brisbane and Darcy was scheduled for surgery to have his cataracts removed. The day of his surgery was terrifying. I had to search into the depths of my soul to trust that the doctors knew what they were doing and were going to fix my little boy. Handing over my tiny little baby was painful; seeing him come back from surgery with patches over his eyes and tubes connected all over him was heartbreaking. A week after his surgery, Darcy was fitted with his first set of contact lenses and he has been wearing lenses ever since. His vision was slow to develop but he is now doing quite well. Since that time we have had two further lots of surgery to fix bilateral strabismus that developed post cataract surgery. He has also developed glaucoma in his right eye – which is apparently a common side effect of cataract surgery. We have made many, many trips back and forward to Brisbane to see the paediatric ophthalmologist who has become more than just a doctor, but a trusted friend who will never give up on trying to give our little boy better vision.

In the midst of the problems with Darcy's eyes we also had heart reviews and endless hearing tests. At three months of age the paediatric cardiologist reviewed Darcy's heart and concluded that he had a "functionally normal heart." The thickening of the pulmonary valve had corrected itself and there were no further issues with his heart. You can imagine the joy at hearing this news. After having such a tough ride with Darcy's eyes, we were so relieved to know that his heart was okay.

Darcy had his first follow-up hearing test when he was only one month old. This was the beginning of a very frustrating journey trying to find out exactly the cause of his hearing problem. It was a very stressful experience as the testing could not be done in our regional town and we had to travel each time we needed to have tests conducted. Each time he was tested he was either too congested to get a true reading or he would not sleep for long enough to test him thoroughly and we would be asked to come back again at a later date. Eventually, Darcy had a hearing test conducted under anaesthetic (during one of his eye surgeries) and he was found to have permanent mild hearing loss in both ears in the high frequency range. This really came as a shock to me and I found myself becoming very emotional when I was told the results. I think I had convinced myself that Darcy would have "glue ear", like many other children with Down syndrome and I was certain that it was something that could be fixed. I had not mentally or emotionally prepared myself for a permanent hearing loss. We decided not to use hearing aids at the time and continued to have Darcy's hearing tested every six months to check that there had not been any changes to his level of hearing and to ensure there were no middle ear problems. Following his check up at 2.5 years of age, the audiologist reported that Darcy had hearing that was adequate for him to develop normal speech and language without the use of hearing aids. That news was music to my ears and I literally jumped for joy when I got home and shared this piece of positive news with Mark.

Not long after Darcy was born, I started joking with doctors that everything about Darcy was "just a little bit not normal". He had a slightly enlarged kidney, but nothing to be concerned about. He had a mild hearing loss, but nothing to be concerned about. His bilirubin levels were just out of the normal range for quite a while, but nothing to be concerned about. He has mild sleep apnoea, but nothing to be concerned about at this stage. His iron levels were often a little bit low, but nothing to be concerned about. His eyes were not perfect, but we were working on it. We had a list of things that were "not quite right" about Darcy and we were certainly kept on our toes trying to stay on top of all the appointments, surgeries, reviews and testing. On top of these minor issues, he had recurrent chest infections and nasal congestion and was hospitalised twice for bronchiolitis and croup. There were times when it felt very unfair that one little person had to go through so much in the first early years of his life, but most of the time we were so incredibly proud of our little boy who handled all the poking and prodding with seemingly unshakable ease.

Darcy is now almost 3 years old and I am pleased to report he has been free from significant health problems for the past six months. The first two years of his life were certainly not easy. We had medical appointments and tests almost every week and quite often the results we received were not good news. It was an emotional rollercoaster. Just as we managed to get on top of one issue, there seemed to be something else come up that rattled our emotions again. There were many times when I wondered "what else" or "how much more" and I felt like I might collapse in a sobbing heap and never get back up again. Sometimes I did collapse in a sobbing heap, but somehow I always managed to get back up. I had to. My two boys needed their Mummy to be strong and they needed their Mummy to look after them. Our challenges are not over. Darcy's eyes are still a "work in progress" and more surgery may be needed to fix the glaucoma. At some stage he may need surgery to have tonsils and adenoids removed to improve his sleep apnoea. Of course, there are the unknowns we can't predict that can come up at any time.

As a family, we are stronger than ever, despite the turbulent couple of years we had with Darcy's health. Every day we are filled with joy as we watch our little boy learn and develop. He and Charlie are so interactive and Darcy watches everything his big brother does and tries to copy him – even climbing onto the coffee table and trying to be superman! We are thrilled to see Darcy reaching milestones that we thought might have been impossible for him, especially as we really had no idea what his vision would be like and how this would affect his ability to do things. Today he is a typical boy who loves his cars and trucks and the outdoors, but who is equally happy to sit and read books snuggled up with his Mummy or Daddy, or draw pictures on the chalkboard. He is charming, very adorable and has a wonderful ability to wrap people around his little finger with just the flash of his smile. Our boys are our world and I can't imagine our lives being any different. I think back to the time when Darcy was first born and I don't think I could have ever pictured back then, just how happy we would be and how wonderful our life would become. What seemed so very difficult in the beginning has now become our "normal" and we love our "normal" life.

~ Allison, Darcy's mum; 34; Queensland, Australia

{Alvaro}

My blood pressure had been high for several hours. The nurse came in, checked my vitals and read my blood pressure to me. It was high again. I made a comment about how high it was and she said, "Its okay, you've been through a lot."

She was referring to the diagnosis I received a few hours earlier. We welcomed our son Alvaro into the world on February 16, 2013 at 6:24am. At 37 weeks I was full term and induced because I was losing my amniotic fluid.

I remember pushing him out with tears in my eyes. They handed him to me. As soon as I started talking to him, this little baby boy stopped crying. It was magical.

Four hours after he was born, the magical feelings were crushed. The pediatrician, after having examined him, asked everyone but the parents to leave the room. With a shaky voice and an apologetic tone she began to explain to us that she believed Alvaro had Down syndrome. In fact, she was 80% sure. She shared with us the markers that led to her suspicions: the low muscle tone, the slanted eyes, and the crease across the palm in his hand.

While my heart was filled with dread and I felt as if the wind knocked out of me, somehow deep inside I knew it to be true. You see, the first fleeting thought in my mind when I held my baby boy was, "This looks like a baby with Down syndrome." I don't know where that thought came from. I had never seen a baby with Down syndrome before. I had only seen older children and individuals with DS. I pushed that fleeting thought from my mind and told myself it was because we had different cultures in our families that he looked different to me.

So here I found myself in the hospital room having been told my son has DS. My blood pressure was sky high for 24 hours. I was in shock. I felt dread. But above all I felt fear. The fear led to questions such as: 'What did this mean for my baby? What did this mean for my family? How could something be so wrong with such a perfect little baby?'

The next few days I experienced confusion, grief, and pain. But I also felt a fierce protectiveness over this little boy's life and body. This was still the same baby who grew inside me. The little boy we'd spent months waiting for. I had to reconcile the boy I went to the hospital to welcome and the little baby boy in my arms with Down syndrome. I reminded myself they were one and the same.

All I could see when I looked at his face was that: Down syndrome. My heart broke that I couldn't see past the diagnosis. I grieved and felt guilt that I wasn't excited and that I felt so sad inside.

A NICU nurse came and spoke with us the day after Alvaro was born. Her own four year old son has DS. Speaking to her was like sunlight shining through the clouds of my heart. My immediate fears were verbalised. Then many of my fears were dispelled. She began to educate me about what a wonderful child Ben was. She shared about her triumphs and even sorrows on her own journey as the parent of a child with Down syndrome. She was a Godsend for me. In the middle of the turmoil in my heart, the seeds of hope, joy, and relief were planted.

Despite the beginning of joy, hope, and relief, I was still processing a gamut of emotions, two of the primary ones being fear and guilt. I experienced a lot of fear and then guilt for all my "negative emotions." I had told myself for years that if I had a baby born with Down syndrome, I'd love him or her just the same. But the reality of the diagnosis stung more than I cared to admit.

I was blessed to have so many supportive friends and family. I was immediately connected with friends of friends who have children with Down syndrome. And luckily, I only received one "We are so sorry and brokenhearted for you," comment. Despite my own personal struggles to accept my life with a new reality, I did not want to be pitied. I wanted to have others love Alvaro for who he was, whether that included 46 or 47 chromosomes. I immediately joined the ranks of those who want their children to be accepted and included with their typical peers.

Equally as scary as an unknown future, was the list of possible health issues Alvaro could possibly have. His first week check-up at his pediatrician's office was met with a long list of specialists Alvaro would need to see to rule out (or find) any of the most common health issues prevalent in individuals with Down syndrome. By the time Alvaro was 6 weeks old, he had received an echogram, had a scheduled appointment with a pediatric Cardiologist, had seen a pediatric Ophthalmologist to check for cataracts, and was evaluated by a Geneticist. I started attending the appointments with my breath held. I received one positive report after another: no cataracts, no major heart condition, good muscle tone, etc. Then, of all things, his jaundice levels started to rise. I was referred to a pediatric Gastroenterologist. The jaundice tests revealed that my son's liver may not be working correctly. He underwent several blood tests and scans to verify that his liver had all the necessary components and checked if it worked as it should. To our great relief, it did. The jaundice began to recede and the possibility of a surgical procedure was taken off the table.

His thyroid levels however, were see-sawing between high and normal levels. We have since seen a pediatric Endocrinologist and he did have high TSH levels which are currently being controlled by medication.

On a social and more personal level, most of my attention was spent settling into a new routine now that I had added a second child to my family. As the days turned into weeks, Alvaro's condition became less and less a focal point. While it remained a reality of my life, it was no longer as important as who he was as a person. His personality began to shine through.

I spent the first few weeks after his birth educating myself about Down syndrome. I read books recommended by friends and the National Down Syndrome Society. I joined a Facebook group for Moms with babies who had DS. I joined the chapter of local Down Syndrome Association. I quickly learned that there were more similarities than differences with DS. Alvaro's extra chromosome just made him extra special. He was not broken. He would live a full and happy life. He may take a little longer to walk or talk, but these were skills he would master. He would be able to go to school, be educated and have a job. He may get married. His potential is NOT limited because he has an extra chromosome.

Because of Facebook and the wonderful sisterhood of fellow mothers of children with T21, Down syndrome became part of my "typical" world. I got to see children every day with Down syndrome. In fact I saw as many, if not more, babies in Alvaro's peer group with Down syndrome than without. Having the ability to share my life, feelings, fears, hopes, and thoughts with these fellow Moms was so important. The support and understanding really helped me in so many ways.

I will be honest also that the first few weeks connecting with these Moms were at times a struggle. So many were so happy and loved their children so well. I was still feeling guilty about my sad feelings. I shared this with them, and again they surrounded me with empathy, support, encouragement, and understanding.

I did have to be careful though how much I spent online. It was easy for me to get excited and scared about all the possible health issues some of the babies were dealing with. I seemed to live online looking up information on ailments such as RSV, Infantile Spasms, and other scary possibilities.

I learned though to just let go and just let Alvaro and his body be our guide to what was going on with him.

By the time Alvaro was four months old, what I thought about when I saw him was simply that he was my son, a joy and a delight. We're lucky that he has had very minimal health issues. He receives physical therapy weekly to work in areas that are physically more challenging for him. Aside from that, I had noticed very little to no difference from my typical son at that age.

Alvaro is one year old now. I have come to wholly accept who he is. In fact, his Down syndrome is just an ingredient in his makeup. Alvaro isn't "my son with Down syndrome." He is simply my son. I do not even think of him as someone with "special needs." I'm not in denial that he is in the special needs categories. It just isn't a label that defines him.

Would I change Alvaro's condition if I could? I don't know. I don't think I would. I would change any health issues that would have negative effects in his body. But I would not change my son. I love him just as he is: beautiful, happy, fun, smart, and well... mine. I am proud and honored to be his mother.

~Rosa, Alvaro's mom; 33; Florida, United States

Blogging @ www.xeeomy.blogspot.com

{Everett}

One would think when you are getting ready to have your fourth child, you would be somewhat prepared, old hat, right? I had a pretty easy pregnancy, some morning sickness but all of our testing and ultrasounds assured us that the baby was doing just fine. I was 38 weeks along

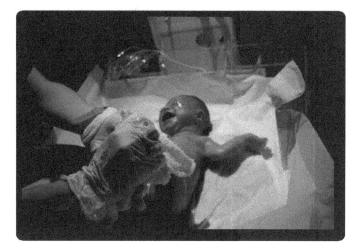

when I had my first contraction at 6am. I foolishly labored (pun intended) under the impression I would have lots of time to prepare and get ready at home. Three short hours later while my husband drove frantically down the highway going 70 mph with me trashing around in the front seat shouting profanities at anyone and anything, I remember thinking I probably shouldn't have made time to shave my legs!

As we pulled up to the hospital, the car hasn't even stopped before I had the door open and I was running to the check-in…well running as fast as anyone can when their contractions are one minute apart! They whisked me up to labor and delivery floor where I got the last open room and met the labor and delivery nurse Beth. I will always remember her lovely blue eyes as she talked to me through the pain and her patience with me as my fear took over.

They eventually were able to give me an epidural but the baby's heart rate was dropping and seemed only happy unless I was flat on my back. Not my optimal laboring position but I made do. The doctor, whom I had never met before, came just in time to deliver the baby, with few quick pushes and a cord that needed to be cut quickly, they brought him up to my chest. I remember seeing him and being in total disbelief! A boy! We finally had a wonderful and precious boy, after three girls, I guess we didn't even think it was possible!

I cuddled him on my chest, he was crying and a bit blue, I looked down at him and asked aloud "What's wrong with his eyes?" They were extremely puffy and oddly shaped but I chalked it up to such a fast and furious labor. The nurses took him to get him weighed and cleaned up a bit while Paul and I joyously called and texted our friends and family members. Neither of us noticed how quiet the room was, how the nurses asked for a pediatrician to come to our room, how the obstetrician left the room in search of one. What I do remember is when he returned.

He took the baby from the nurses and placed him in my arms bundled in his blanket and with stocking cap that all newborn babies seem to wear as a rite of passage. Paul looked over my shoulder, both of us still in amazement we had a baby boy.

The doctor looked at me and said kindly "I want you to tell me what you notice about your son." I didn't hesitate a moment. As I stared at the bundle in my arms, my eyes filled with tears and my heart began to hammer in my chest. I immediately replied "His ears are low set and his eyes are close together, he has Down syndrome, doesn't he?" The room was utterly silent as I began to sob.

Everyone was obviously shocked I saw it so quickly. "I'm an obstetrician, not a pediatrician but yes, I believe he does based on some of his features." The nurses' eyes were filled with tears.

I don't remember looking at Paul, but he tells me he just was in an utter state of disbelief because the baby looked so 'normal' to him. He did not see what I saw. Know what I already knew in my heart. He began to cry with me.

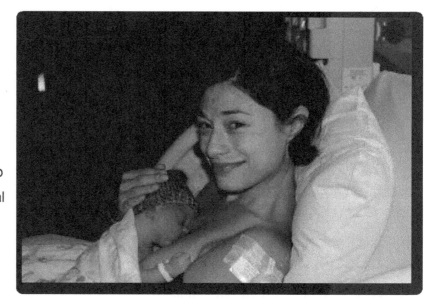

I pulled the baby tightly to my chest and said "Oh, my sweet, special baby boy, we are going to love you" as my sobs and tears grew. I will always cling to the fact this was my first visceral response to the news because what feelings came next. Feelings that I am ashamed to admit I had.

I don't know if I can ever truly describe the emotions. I went from such elation to complete and utter devastation in the space of a second. Just typing these words causes such an exquisite ache in my chest and tightening in my throat, so hard to put into words and onto paper and to be honest and remember.

My whole body was numb, I felt no pain other the searing hole left in chest where my heart used to be. Shock, pain, disbelief, devastation all blended together, the joy was gone.

My husband took a picture, as I told him we needed to have a photo of me smiling, because what would he think one day looking at his baby book if there were no smile.

The pediatrician came into the room; she was a kind lady who examined the baby. She explained she would be sending a chromosome test to check the baby for Trisomy 21. She pointed out the traits that indicated to her he had this condition. His eyes have the epicanthal folds, lows set ears that are slightly folded over, a sandal toe gap (a space between the big toe and the next). A small placenta also correlates with Down syndrome which I had. She did comment that he had good muscle tone and was pleased he seemed to be nursing well.

How could this have happened? I was furious and felt utterly betrayed the medical people who cared for me during pregnancy. I had the testing which showed my risk was normal and my prenatal testing and high level ultrasound was normal. I was only 33 when we conceived. I raged against the world, this was not real, there was a mistake. This was a horrible nightmare, this happens to other people. Not to me. Not to MY family.

What I am about to admit are shameful, despicable feelings and thoughts. I'm sure others will judge me but it is real and my truth and my story.

I vaguely remember moving from the labor and delivery suite to the mom and baby room. I was pushed in a wheelchair as I held the baby in my arms. My eyes were swollen and tears flowed down my cheeks. I kept the baby pressed to my chest; I didn't want anyone to see him. People averted their eyes as I rolled past. I saw their eyes as they looked at my face and how their glances would slide off into the distance. I was holding a baby but something was wrong. The nurses at the station all knew, I could see it.

We got settled in the new room, the baby was in the bassinet to my left between the bed and the window. I couldn't even look at him. He wasn't a baby to me, I didn't know what he was.

I was alone in the room as Paul left to get my mother at the airport, the sun was setting and the room grew dark. At that moment the vilest thoughts crossed my mind. I did NOT want him. Was there a way to place him up for adoption? But then what I would tell the girls? What if he died and I had to bury him? I didn't want him alive; I wanted a 'normal' baby, not this thing- this imperfect thing with funny looking eyes and ears. He would never leave our home, he would have an awkward looking body, he would be made fun of, as would our other kids. I would spend the rest of my life taking care of him. I would have no life of my own. He would never live on his own. He would never play basketball in high school like his dad, never drive, never go to college, and never marry. The list went on and on in my head...

I cried and sobbed for hours straight, alone in that room except for that baby. The pain and sadness exploded, my body was wracked with grief and pain- grieving for a child I had lost and despising the one had. I'm sure whoever passed my room must have thought the baby had died in childbirth by my sobs, little did they know it was just a mom who was wishing for it. As the room became dark and my head hurt and my eyes were so swollen I could barely see, I couldn't even look at him, as I rejected him. I look back at that night and the days that followed, his NICU stay, his heart defect diagnosis and a subsequent hospitalization and I wonder how I could have had those callous, horrific feelings. What kind of mother was I?

What kind of person was I? I suppose time has allowed me to be kinder to myself. I regret my feelings, but it was the journey I took. My best role models were my three little girls who welcomed and loved their brother without any hesitation. Complete and utter lover, no reservations.

I guess I need to be kind to myself. I knew nothing of Down syndrome, I never met anyone with it. I think my lack of knowledge and the lack of information that came with his birth left me paralyzed. I had all these ideas of what it would mean, but I realize now, 19 months later, I was so wrong. He is a survivor and fighter. Everett will have a life worth living and will make an impact. He is not suffering. He is perfect. He is normal. He is thriving and teaching me every day what it truly means to love.

~ Amber, Everett's mom; 34; Colorado, United States

{Thea}

It was anything but ordinary. My husband and I anticipated this day with much excitement—having a home visit a week before with our midwife where we finalized the plan to have our little child at the local birth center. Labor started and continued quickly at home, after some time laboring at home it was time to make our way to the birth center. Upon arrival our excitement continued; we had been waiting for this day for nine long months and it was finally here: the day

to meet our first child. Plans changed quickly, very quickly when it was determined that I was fully dilated and baby was breech; to be exact our little one was footling breach. Our excitement deflated when we were transported to a local hospital by ambulance. Labor pains continued but I was instructed to ignore the endless urges to push while being inundated with endless medical professionals rambling off question after question. An emergency C-section was scheduled soon after we arrived. The sterile operation began, and I was placed in a hospital gown despite my request to remain in regular clothes; I was told it was not an option. Endless thoughts circled my brain—this was definitely not "the plan" but I was comforted with the thoughts that it won't be long and we'll be

united with our little child soon, very soon. Sure enough, she arrived. I was able to see her seconds after the delivery as a nurse positioned a mirror and my spouse announced that baby was a girl! My intuition was right – a little girl as I had expected for much of my pregnancy. I still can't explain exactly what gave "it" (Down Syndrome) away but I knew the second I saw her. Or I thought I knew; my brain was flooded. I was alone on the operating table. I was numb, completely numb, both emotionally and physically. The wait in the recovery room was the longest two hours of my life. I couldn't begin to process anything with the combination of the pain medication, the exhaustion, and the uncertainty. Physically, my body shook. I was finally reunited with my spouse and we didn't have to say anything but we wept together because we were overwhelmed. The next 3 ½ days were much of a blur—many of the events ran together:

numerous consultations, blood draws, screenings and tests, and tears both of joy and sadness. A resident gave us the diagnosis of Down syndrome the day after her birth. The resident angered me, saying senseless things by categorizing my child. I thought many, many times "give her a chance, she is unique and she is my child." Despite all the questions and worries, I had a calming moment as our baby looked up at me with her beautiful little eyes—she reassured me that she was going to be okay. She is our little warrior and she will accomplish many, many things.

During those first few days of life we learned of Thea's heart defect. We were told she had a "large" VSD. Despite the physician whom gave us the initial Down syndrome diagnosis the rest of the medical team were supportive. During the hospital stay the time of her heart surgery was unknown; but ideally the team estimated the surgery would be around 6 months of age. We had regular monthly visits to monitor her growth, heart murmur development and weight gain.

Ultimately, the team decided to surgery was better completed earlier than later. Thea was scheduled for surgery just before she turned three months; she only weight 7lbs 8oz. Still a peanut. Surgery to this day, this the most difficult thing I have been through. The preparation, the team taking her and the waiting…and waiting. Hourly updates were helpful but we just wanted to be reunited with her. She showed her strengthen, after 7 hours of surgery she had her 3 holes repaired; 2 ASDs, 1 VSD and a closure of the PDA. A warrior. I don't think anything can prepare a parent to seeing a child following OHS; it's hard, devastating, a feeling of helplessness. Recovery, happened. It was the longest 12 days in that CICU (cardiac ICU). I didn't' think it was ever going t end. There was progress but setbacks; infection, a clasped lung, but day by day she gained strength. The warrior shined through. We have had our number of medical appointments and visits with ENT/audiologist, ophthalmologist, swallow study, cardiologist follow-ups, endocrinologist. But bless her soul; she is strong and health. Only once has she been prescribed antibiotics in her the first 17 months of her life.

Thea is now almost 18 month; and she truly is such an incredible child. Honestly, I wouldn't change a thing about my girl. Some days, I do worry; but worrying is expected for any parent. I probably worry more some days and I am okay with that. What worry me most are stereotypes and stigmas. It's time to open the world to what is the truth. I am working on it- one day at a time…everyday!

Thea is the child we always wanted. She is feisty and has a happy, hearty-soul. She makes our days brighter. I have no doubt she will be an amazing little girl and will continue to surprise us with all her accomplishments. She has already brought so much joy to our home and hearts. And she will definitely continue!

~Kate, Thea's mom; 30; Wisconsin, United States

{Zoey}

Defining moments.

When I look back over the past nine months this is the phrase the most often comes to mind. There is now a definite line in the sand. Before Zoey and after. I have long known the before - it's the after that had me scared to death.

In all honesty I did not know much about Down syndrome. I just knew it was the thing I was often warned about as a complication as I grew older at my yearly OBGYN visits. As I approached 30 it felt like this was just cause to create some urgency in starting a family.

Growing up I didn't really know anyone with Down syndrome. We had a summer camp hosted at our local high school for young adults with different developmental disabilities. Some of my friends volunteered that week and I remember really admiring them for that, personally I felt a bit

uncomfortable. I was so afraid of having anyone think I was "talking down" to them, I just didn't want to insult anyone and for that I shied away. I was ignorant and nervous about stepping out of my comfort zone.

Fast forward to present day, I was 35 years old and pregnant with my third baby. I had had a 2nd trimester miscarriage with my previous pregnancy so while this pregnancy was turning out to be uneventful I was often on edge. I frequently asked baby for some reassurance and she was always willing to oblige with some hearty kicks.

As my due date came and went I wasn't too worried. I had gone over with my previous pregnancies so I felt this was just routine. My doctor had me undergo a biophysical exam, followed my a non-stress test because baby didn't want to do her practice breathing. Two days later same tests were repeated with the same result. The reason I mention this was because immediately after I delivered she didn't cry hard - I was so worried she wasn't breathing - I must have asked a million times if she was ok. Looking back I should have known something was going on. The room was much too quiet. There were too many people there. No one congratulated us on the birth of our baby. Nobody said we had a healthy baby girl. No one was talking, the room was so quiet, and looks avoided.

The most remarkable times in my life have been the birth of my children Jack and Maya, I felt joy like I never knew existed, like my heart might just explode with happiness. Zoey's birth was different.

I had a very rapid delivery and had a terrible migraine immediately following delivery. I was able to hold her for a few moments before they whisked her away to the NICU. At this point I wasn't too concerned. She was breathing on her own after all. I remember looking at her and thought "huh ... something seems different?" But soon she was gone and my family and I were laughing and joking about that crazy delivery.

Not long after the doctor walked in and I knew something was wrong, I could tell whatever he was about to say was something paining even his heart. I will never forget those moments. I will never forget the detail. I will never forget how the doctor spoke softly but yet with concern. Down syndrome.

This must be some kind of nightmare. Please God please wake me up! This can't be happening, this can't be real. This CAN'T be happening! I felt heartache like I had never known. It was the most devastating sadness. Sadness and heartache so intense, so very intense, so cutting. I couldn't breathe, the weight was so heavy. I clung to my husband and sobbed. Still praying for this to be some kind of nightmare. We were in shock. I felt numb.

It seemed like forever till we were able to go see her. It felt strange. I was nervous to see her. How was I going to react. I mean I still loved this baby right? Yet everything felt different. I just had a baby, where was the happiness? Instead it was replaced with instructions on NICU protocol, my baby covered in wires and tubes, and immense fear. She didn't look like my baby, this didn't feel like my baby. I hurt so desperately. I looked and looked at her and touched her soft skin. "Why God?" I hate to admit I questioned 'Why us?' Why were we being punished? I feel terrible for those feelings now, but I want to add these details because somewhere someone else may be going through the same emotions – and it's okay. I know its seems so hard right now but you will pick yourself up and do this. You will find love for your little one that is more powerful then anything you could ever imagine.

Joy has returned. It was there all along but my own worry, fear and ignorance were in the way. I

say "Defining Moments" because it has all changed. My role as mom has changed, my relationship with God has changed, my outlook on life has changed. Everything changed – changed for the better. I feel my own life has taken on such focus – advocate and educater.

I recently read a quote "If you believe in something with all your heart, then fight for it with all your might."* And I believe in Zoey.

~Jackie, Zoey's mom; 35; North Dakota, United States

*sevenly.org (quote source)

{Aiden}

To tell you our story I will have to take you back to the part when we decided it was time to bring a baby into our lives. I had always dreamed of being a mother, raising my children with my husband by my side. A baby was all I could think about and over the next fourteen months we discovered just how difficult it was to get the timing right. After one heart breaking miscarriage I was pregnant with Aiden. During the next nine months I day dreamed about who he might look like, I just wanted him to be perfect in every way. Than strangely on the other hand I would day dream about how I would cope if he was born with a disability and think about how that would impact on our daily lives.

Strange as this may sound I think I did this as a way to prepare myself for the unexpected. As I always had this feeling something wasn't quite right even though the midwives reassured me at every appointment that he looked perfectly fine. But no matter what I just couldn't shake the feeling. I guess you might call it mother's intuition. I remember one visit in particular with my midwives when I brought up the nuchal translucency scan. She was surprised I asked about it and reassured me that I was low risk due to my age and no family history. She informed me I had only a three day window left to get the ultrasound done. The next day I was straight on the phone calling all the scan places though no one could fit me in. I still the remember the phone

conversation I had that day with my husband. I told him I couldn't get the appointment, then I asked him, "It will be alright wont it? Like the midwife said we are too young to have a baby with Down syndrome". He responded confidently,

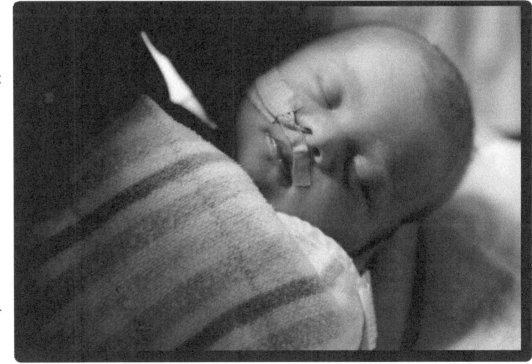

"Yeah of course it will be ok". Then that was the end of that. Looking back I believe God intervened here as we were both adamant from our previous discussion that we didn't want to bring a child with a disability into this cruel world. It would be too heart breaking to see them struggle and suffer. Little did I know that that's not what life would be like with Aiden.

Finally the day arrived a little earlier than expected at 36 weeks. I was more excited about going into labour than scared of what was to come. I called all my family while pacing excitedly and breathing through each contraction. I kept focused in the beginning by reminding myself that each contraction was bringing me closer to holding my baby for first time. After eight hours of what I described as the most horrific pain I have ever felt I finally saw my little man for the first time. Feeling his warm slippery body on my chest was surreal. I gently kissed his forehead in complete awe that this baby somehow fitted inside me and now here he is. Then they whisked him away.

Still in a daze from the birthing experience I was being attended to by my nurse while the other was looking Aiden over doing the usual assessments. Out of nowhere she announced, "I am going to call in the paediatrician because he looks a little floppy." Little did I know how my world was about to be tipped upside down and my path in life changed forever. I remember the paediatrician announcing to the room, "He has features of trisomy 21". I looked around the room at my family's' worried faces and my husband asked him what that meant. He responded with, "Down syndrome". I questioned him disbelieving his words, "Are you ever wrong?" In a cold, definite tone he stated, "No" and marched out of the room. In that moment I felt myself detach from reality and in my head all these images of what I thought Down syndrome to be flashed in my mind. The almond eyes I knew but I had images of adults not being able to walk, talk or function. Then a thought crossed my mind that this baby who will grow to be an adult will now be living with us for the rest of his life. He will need twenty-four - seven care right through his adult years. Selfishly I kept thinking I will never have a life with just me and my husband again and that's if we even survive this. I felt myself go numb and cold inside. Then it was my turn to hold him and I reluctantly did. He looked peaceful all wrapped up in his stripped hospital blanket. I stared at him thinking this isn't what I wanted over and over again. In that moment I disowned him and handed him to who ever wanted him, I just knew it wasn't me. Looking back I wished that the doctors would have let me have my bonding time first before they dropped the bomb on us that night. I couldn't help but wonder if this would have changed my post natal experience with Aiden.

That night the nurses kindly rearranged the rooms so my husband could stay with me. All night I laid in bed awake waiting for the sun to come up and for it all to be a mistake. Getting the confirmation the next morning was earth shattering. I was overwhelmed with grief for the baby I had imagined had lost and for the one who now took its place. Despite my worries from the moment Aiden was born my husband was a proud loving dad who only saw a helpless little baby who needed our love and support. He stayed by his bedside until I had the strength to face reality and visit him in the special care nursery the next morning. He was my rock through the most difficult time in my life and this only strengthened our bond as a couple.

Over the next week Aiden was transferred between hospitals as they discovered he had two holes in his heart (complete AVSD) and the doctors explained that he would stay in hospital until he either went into heart failure or began putting on weight but surgery was inevitable. As the weeks passed his condition continued to deteriorate despite the doctors best efforts. That time in hospital I spent every day with him trying to form an attachment. I bathed him, cuddled him, talked to him and when no one was around quietly sung him songs. Truthfully I felt like an actor pretending to be this loving mother but all I felt was numb inside.

I was adamant that I wanted to try to breastfeed Aiden as we all thought it would be a great bonding experience for the both of us. Despite my efforts Aiden had trouble latching due to the low muscle tone then as his condition deteriorated so did his ability to stay awake and feed. At four weeks old he was transferred to the children's hospital and three days later I reluctantly handed my vulnerable little man over to the heart surgeons. It was in that moment I realised I didn't want to let him go. I broke down in an uncontrollable sob and truthfully this surprised me. That day I prayed to God "I do want him, I will love him, I don't care that he has Down syndrome. I'm sorry I didn't realise it at the start but please help him get through this". Just in case God didn't hear me the first time I repeated it over and over again in that waiting room. The second the pager beeped my entire family all jumped up at once and raced to the door to hear the good news that the surgery was a success.

Looking at Aiden for the first time with all the wires and tubes was confronting and scary. He was swollen and looked nothing like the little man that I held that morning. Over the following week he was weaned off his medications, oxygen and began tolerating tube feeds again. Slowly his swelling went down and after a few scares and six weeks in hospital from his birth day it was time to go home. Naively I thought the worst was over but little did I know the challenges that lay ahead for both me and Aiden.

That time at home I was overwhelmed with administering his heart medications, specialist visits, therapies, dealing with his range of health issues and sicknesses plus on top of this processing all the information I could find relating to Down syndrome. It wasn't long until it was obvious to my friends and family that I was depressed and not coping. With my families support and encouragement I sought the help I needed and finally I saw the light at the end of a very dark tunnel. I remember the time when it all changed for me. Aiden was eight months old laughing and giggling in his cot. I picked him up and for the first time I felt a surge of love inside me. In that moment I fell in love and began to feel again. I finally began to feel proud to have my little man and began to see him as a baby first and his diagnosis second. Overtime I no longer saw the Down syndrome when I looked at him and I eventually stopped thinking about it constantly. To us Aiden is just Aiden.

We feel so lucky and blessed that he chose us to be his parents. He brings so much joy and laughter to our lives. He means the world to our families and we would never wish to change him or our journey. I know our future will be challenging with many ups and downs but now I am not scared. I am excited to see him grow and develop into a young man. We are just thankful to have him here with us and whatever the future holds we will face it together as a family. If I could go back in time I would tell myself back then that life now with Aiden is difficult at times but most of all it is full of happiness and laughter. He is perfect and exactly what you wanted plus more, you just don't realise it yet.

It has taken me four years since his diagnosis to write my story. This is the first time I haven't cried reliving those painful memories of our first year. I used to feel guilty about my feelings in the start and how I reacted. I found it hard to share these deep dark feelings with anyone but now I have realised it's not about where you start, it's about the journey and where you end up that's important....love and acceptance. Now instead of feeling a great sense of burden that I will always have to care for him I feel lucky that he will always be close by perhaps even out the back in the granny flat. But whatever the case I hope he is never too far away.

Aiden is a thriving, cheeky, strong willed four and half year old little man. His fun loving personality is infectious with not only family and friends but strangers we meet on our daily journeys. He starts at special needs school next year and is talking two to three word sentences. He loves exploring outside and being overly rough with his younger brother. This year he has been healthy with no trips to hospital or sicknesses. All the specialist visits have slowed right down and life finally feels normal. It's been a tough journey but he is definitely worth every minute of it.

~Michelle, Aiden's mum; 25; NSW, Australia

{Eden}

When I think about the day we got Eden's diagnosis, there is no one word to explain it. It is like a million tiny air bubbles, each with a different emotion or thought, effervescing to the surface of reality. Some thoughts sting, some are sweet, and you just cannot take them all in at once.

We received her diagnosis at birth, but to understand the place I was in, I have to provide a little background of my pregnancy first.

I met my husband in a whirlwind of romance in 2009. In 2010, we lost our first child to an early miscarriage. But in 2011, I found out I was pregnant again just after our 1 year wedding anniversary! We were so ready to do everything right, and that included taking any options offered to us such as pre-natal testing, even though I didn't exactly know what that was at the time. After my 12 week ultra-sound/NT scan and first trimester blood tests, I sat alone in the waiting room filled with every confidence in the world. After one miscarriage, I figured this was my turn to have the perfect pregnancy! I've rarely ever been sick. I like to think I

take good care of myself. And I'm pretty lucky most of the time—that's just how my life works. Everything was falling perfectly in place.

After quite a long time of fumbling with the blood test numbers, the doctors at the testing center were able to present me with first trimester screen that just cleared the "normal range" for someone my age [for a Down syndrome pregnancy]. (1:336) They wrote down some dates I could come in for an amnio, but invasive testing was never in my plan. So I opted just to come back for the Quad Screen (to complete the sequential screening), hoping to set my mind at ease. Weeks went by. My pregnancy stayed right on track. And I called to check the results of the Quad screen at about 18 weeks. "1:560" the nurse let me know. This pregnancy was now officially "normal."

Our 20-week anatomy scan looked great, and we found out we were having a baby girl! My only complications were nerve-related pain, but everything with our baby girl checked out perfectly every time. She had a strong heartbeat, and she even used to kick the heartbeat monitor they put on my belly—which prompted the nurse practitioner to tell me that meant she was "smart". Ten days before my due date, on the weekend of a full-moon (just as I had predicted), my water broke at on a Saturday morning. By 10pm we were at the hospital, and labor was on!

Our sweet baby girl was born at 4:56am on a Sunday. She was placed on my chest with wide-open doe-eyes, flanked by long lashes, and she looked right into my eyes with tiny expression of wonder. In those first few moments, I will admit that I had a sense that something about her was *different*. But I had certainly never seen a baby that brand new, so I quickly pushed any uneasy thoughts to the back of my mind. I kept her close to me for a few minutes before I

relinquished her to my husband who carried her to the nursery with the nurse.

When my husband returned, I started to get up to get myself together, and that's when the pediatrician on call stepped in. He said he wanted to talk to us "about the baby," but the tone in which he said that was off. I was already feeling horribly guilty for taking the pain medicine, and I was expecting to get a scolding for that. But he began to go through a list of her features and finally said, "It looks like we have a Downs baby." I just stood there, part of my brain thinking that he *must* be wrong because that was not what the tests said and part of my brain already knowing that he just verbalized what I went through my mind earlier that morning. I was sad, scared, angry at the doctor, apologetic to my husband—I felt like I had failed him. But that's when my husband hugged me and said, "God must have thought this little girl needed some awesome parents."

We hugged a little while longer, and he asked me if I wanted to stay in the room a bit more. But the next thing I remember saying was that I was ready "to get dressed and get tough." She needed us. And we didn't know if yet, but we needed her too.

~ Sheri; Eden's mom; 35; Tennessee

On Twitte:r @xinefly

{Henry}

I came home worn out from the long week of work. My ever-growing belly was now at 38 weeks, and I was slowing down. I woke up Saturday morning, feeling rested and refreshed. We went about our day, going for groceries and taking our dog for a walk through the winding streets of our neighborhood. The weather was beautiful and the contractions started coming, with Charlie studiously timing them.

As the night came and went, time got fuzzy and the pain intensified, until we decided to go to the hospital at 6:00am.

The triage nurse then checked me for dilation, and I was at a 9, so was immediately wheeled

me into L&D to start pushing. My OB materialized, and no more waiting! I could feel the baby moving, and I changed positions until I found one that worked.

I caught my breath one more time and pushed as hard as I could, screaming the whole time. "Fire, fire, fire!'

and then relief, as his head, then shoulders came out. He was here at last! Our Henry. I listened desperately for his cry, which came loud and clear and mad. I heard Apgar scores of 9's in the background and sobbed with happiness and relief. We were safely on the other side.

The nurses put him right on my chest, wide awake, with deep, dark blue eyes. His poor head was coned from all the pushing but I didn't care. He was perfect. He looked right at me almost curiously, studying. I gingerly touched his spiky tuft of blonde hair, his narrow shoulders, and kissed him. He was so warm. I held him to me, bringing him to my breast. He looked up at me and tried to suck. He was just a little small, still, to latch, but he licked and tried. Proudly, I exclaimed "My smart baby, you know what to do!"

The nurse later asked Charlie if he wanted to hold his son, wrapped up in the pink- and green-striped swaddling cloth. He took Henry from me nervously, and leaned down to him. "I'm your daddy, do you know me?" I cried again. We grabbed our iPhones and I snapped a picture of Henry with his dad and we started texting and calling, getting the news out. The room quietly emptied out.

We moved to the comfortable Recovery room, which already had 'Welcome to the world Henry Joseph!' scribbled on the whiteboard. The sun shone and we couldn't stop staring at our boy. Henry loved cuddling with both of us, but we were still struggling with breast feeding. I asked for a lactation consultant to come in because he still wasn't latching, but I'd read somewhere it would take practice and time for my milk to come in. The University of Michigan basketball game came on at noon, and Charlie watched the game with Henry sleeping in his arms. He was the happiest I'd ever seen him. I slept for the first time since he was born.

The pediatrician came for his rounds at 2pm. He greeted us and took Henry gingerly from Charlie's arms, and laid him on the examination table. He moved Henry's limbs, checking for flexibility. He picked Henry up to see how strong his neck was. I looked at my firstborn being handled and then impatiently at the doctor, just wanting my baby back.

He quietly handed Henry back to me and I was only half listening as he began to talk. I already knew what he was going to say, that Henry is perfect, and focused all my attention on my baby. "Did you know Henry was going to be a boy?"

"Yup!" I said proudly. "We could tell right away at the ultrasound."

"You had an ultrasound?" he asked, almost sharply.

Cluelessly, I answered again happily, looking only at Henry, "Oh, yes. We had one done at 19 weeks."

He cleared his throat and started speaking again.

"The nurses noted some characteristics that led them to believe there is a possibility that your son has Down syndrome..."

I finally looked up at him, holding Henry protectively as he continued.

"Henry has smaller, lower set ears, and his tongue protrudes somewhat. There is a gap between his big toe and his other toes and he may have folds on his eyelids. I've looked at him and can't quite be sure, though. Usually babies with Down syndrome have low muscle tone and he doesn't. There is often a single crease on the palm of the hand, but I don't see that with him."

"Babies with Down syndrome may have heart issues. I didn't hear a heart murmur at all, which is a good sign, but in order to confirm he's okay we'll need to do an echocardiogram on him right away. The most common defects are ASDs and VSDs, and there are ways to fix them if Henry has either of these."

"Again, it's hard for me to tell. The nurses noticed it but I don't see it so clearly. The only way to know for sure is to get a sample for a karyotype to count the number of chromosomes. I just don't think it's fair to take this without telling the parents. In case it is positive they should be prepared."

My mind raced and I was very still as I was taking this in. The important thing was not to scare Henry - or the doctor. I wanted to handle this well. I thought quickly...The nurses are who noticed first. They see so many babies, they usually are right because they have all that experience... Still, Henry probably didn't have any heart problems. The doctor even said so.

I held Henry tight and trained my eyes on the doctor. He was uncomfortable. That wasn't a good sign either. My stomach started to feel dread. Still, there was only a possibility. Maybe just a ten percent risk. And I'm so lucky. There's no way this will turn out bad in the end. I'm so very lucky. Very soon I'll be out of the hospital and remember this as a scare.

I didn't speak, but eventually heard Charlie's clear voice, behind me. God, I was so relieved. I couldn't even think to ask any questions, and was so thankful he could.

"When you say 'a chance', what does that mean? What percentage would you give it?"

The doctor cleared his throat and said, "Fifty-fifty, maybe."

I stopped breathing, and remained very still, as my mind flew. ...Fifty-fifty is too big. No. No. It's just too much of a chance, a flip of a coin for my son's future? It's not that maybe he has Down syndrome anymore, it's that maybe he doesn't...

I looked down at Henry, trying to shut the doctor out. The room grew, the doctor seemed to retreat, and Henry and I shrank together, everything seeming too massive. I heard Charlie's voice again, far behind me this time. Not even a second had gone by but the world was completely different.

"This conversation doesn't feel like fifty-fifty. Would you put money on it?"

The doctor paused and looked at us, assessing. Then, simply:

"I'd put money on it."

The conversation continued, quietly, with us grilling the doctor. What did ASD and VSD stand for? We needed to research. And then it was over, the sun was setting in the warm winter. He promised to come back tomorrow, to check on us. On his way out, our pediatrician stopped.

"The most important thing right now is that you treat him just like you would for any baby. He needs the same food and care and love that any other baby does."

Well duh. Of course I would treat him the same. Still, it was a relief to hear.

We were alone now. The room started out silent, with me on the hospital bed holding Henry and Charlie in the father's corner, both researching furiously on our phones. We both stared at Henry, trying to reconcile him with the images of babies with Down syndrome on the Internet.

I found the statistics, that about 1 in every 750-800 babies born to women my age have Down syndrome, and started scanning everybody that I knew who had a baby. I was the only one. A new parents guide online had a question on if the assessments from doctors were ever found to be wrong once the karyotype was back. The answer was no, that it was incredibly rare. So, that was it then. No more denial, it wasn't a 50-50 shot. It wasn't even an "I'd put my money on it." It was pretty much a certainty. Even in the dusk, looking down at Henry in my arms, his ear was a little too folded. Everything else I could explain away, but the ear. All of it together just added up. And why wouldn't it be me, us? It only makes sense. Statistically someone will be the one out of 800.

Charlie was over in the father's area coming to the same conclusion. I had family friends that had a daughter with Ds, so the questions started, raining on top of me. How much did I know? What were her limitations? Could she play sports? Read? Talk? Then came the most important questions. "Is she happy? Are her parents happy?"

I thought about it honestly. Well, yes, she is happy. I used to go to her basketball games. She could talk, and walk, and play sports. Her parents are very happy, still in love after all these years. I looked at Charlie and firmly stated "This is not a tragedy. This is just something we didn't pick." He agreed again, and we changed Henry together.

Charlie said he was going to talk to the pediatrician tomorrow, to tell him that we understood what it all meant and that we were fine. At least that way we could get our cards on the table without being patronized.

After feeding Henry and gently placing him in his bassinet, I got a heavy heart again. I crawled out of the hospital bed and over to the father's futon area, near the window. It was dark now, and we clung to each other, crying at times. He was hooked up to wires to check his heart and too small and tired to breastfeed. Everybody would know. All of our friends, everybody at work, would find out and pity us, gossip about him.

I deserved this, somehow. I was so proud of myself the whole pregnancy for giving Charlie a healthy baby. I crawled into the shower and as it started to warm up, my insides ached and I began wracking with sobs. I went from having everything I'd ever dreamed of and lost it all, all within hours.

Why did it have to be my son? He's innocent, perfect. He didn't do anything to deserve this. Why is it him and not me?

I racked my brain stupidly, trying desperately to offer something that would help. A trade. I'd offer myself for him to be normal. I knew even as I was thinking that it was useless. I couldn't give anybody anything that could help. I was completely helpless. I had absolutely nothing to offer. Charlie wouldn't want us anymore. He would be ashamed of us.

I stayed in the shower a long time, willing the water to wash away my grief. My routine helped, shampoo, conditioner, face wash, body wash, towel dry, lotion. My nice clean warm clothes in place of my bloody robe. It was a first step towards normalcy.

And after this, Henry slept soundly, curling into me, trusting me. Suddenly I was ashamed. I had to protect Henry from the world, even me. He is my baby, and I wasn't going to let him down ever again. He was healthy and handsome and just the baby I asked for, and we vowed not to ever take him for granted. I climbed back in the oversized bed, cuddling with Henry again to soothe me, and Charlie soon joined us both. When we were with him it was all so much easier. He was just our son and we were his mommy and daddy.

Today Henry is a happy, thriving 19 month old! He is standing all by himself and already taking a few steps! He toddles around the house holding my hand looking for his doggie and eating Cheerios off the floor. He breastfed until he started solids at 6 months old, and his favorite foods are avocado and pasta. Every day he kisses and tickles his mommy and daddy, plays with his elephant and ring toys, stacks his blocks, and helps us play music and read books. He uses about 15 signs with us, showing us trees, fish, and telling us when he wants food or is 'all done'!

He is handsome, smart, loving, and wonderful, and best known for his white blonde Mohawk and his amazing smile. He is truly the most fun little boy I could dream of having, and I wouldn't trade one moment with him for the world. We were made to be his parents and Henry to be our son, and the more we grow together the more I realize how lucky we are! He's already taught me more about life, love, and happiness than I ever thought possible!

~ Shawn, Henry's mom; 32; North Carolina, United States

{Camden}

I was walking to Starbucks at work with a friend and I was talking about my 20 week sonogram coming up. "I can't wait for this appointment because I have been worried about Down syndrome". I don't know why I said it, but it was true. I declined all prenatal testing even though with my first I did them all. Fast forward to being 28 weeks pregnant and I'm in the hospital. My water had broke and I was on bed rest hoping to wait it out until 34 weeks. A perinatologist comes in to do a detailed sonogram. "Did your OB ever mention anything about Down syndrome?" I kind of froze and just answered "no, why? Do you see something?" She said she saw nothing in particular and it was not discussed further. I would stay on bed rest in the hospital for approximately three more weeks before Camden would make his appearance. I never thought about Down syndrome again. I put it out of my mind.

At 31 weeks a c-section was scheduled since baby boy decided he was ready. I remember that Monday as if it were yesterday. It was November 26th at 7:00 am. The nurse who would

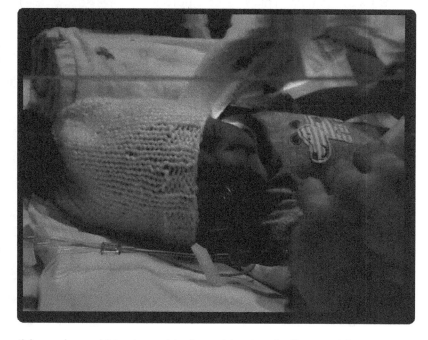

accompany me would be the first nurse I had at admission three weeks earlier. I hadn't seen her since then. This was my first c-section so the nerves were high. I remember my husband sitting by my side holding my hand still because I was shaking uncontrollably. It took only minutes and I hear the doctor say, "Here he comes". I start whispering "Please let him cry, please let him cry" over and over again. He's not supposed to be here this early and I just want to hear him cry. In the next few seconds I hear the angelic sound of my baby boy's cries. Sighs of relief and tears come soon after. I get a glimpse of him before they wheel him away to the NICU. My husband would accompany him while they finish up with me in the OR. After what felt like a lifetime I was taken to the NICU to see my boy. He was perfect. He was breathing on his own and doing fantastic. They put him on my chest and I just closed my eyes and held him. The next few seconds would shatter my perfect moment with my boy. The doctor came over to explain what wouldl happen during his stay in the NICU. Then he said, "We are sending off some tests because of his dysmorphic facial features". Huh? I was still in a bit of a haze due to medications and I didn't

even think to ask him anything else before he disappeared. So I then turn to the nurse and ask her what he was talking about. She tells me that they suspect he has Down syndrome. It still didn't register in my brain. That couldn't be right. Everything has been fine up until now. She told me it would take a week to get the results back and not to worry. I have heard when a physician suspects a newborn has DS that they are right about 90% of the time. This was so different because it was more like 50/50. I'm half Korean which means Camden is a quarter. So a lot of the nurses (and even doctors) thought it was just the Asian features. One doctor even told me not to worry because she doubts he has it. So, I didn't really worry about it. In fact, my husband and I put it out of our minds because it didn't seem possible.

Exactly one week later on December 3, 2012, I heard the words that would change our lives forever. "I'm sorry mom, he does have it". I can't describe the pain that goes through you. It's as if she told me my child was gone. I couldn't see because there were so many tears. I remember putting my baby boy back in his isolette and walking out of the NICU broken hearted. I called my husband since he was not with me. He was two hours away back at home working. I don't recall much about the conversation as we were both devastated. We didn't even talk the next two days. I will always remember when my husband came to see us after those two days and the first words out of his mouth when he pulled up were, "I'm excited. This is gonna be good". That was the moment I knew we would be okay...more than okay.

Camden is a healthy, happy, thriving and stubborn 9 month old today. All the medical appointments have slowed down and we are enjoying each and every moment with our sweet boy. His personality is really starting to shine through. His whole face lights up when he smiles and he lets you know (very loudly) when no one is giving him any attention. He is definitely a daddy's boy as daddy spoils him rotten. We are working on sitting, rolling, and crawling. We just started using sign language videos and he seems to really enjoy them! We are excited about what the future holds and I can tell you that this amazing boy has changed our lives in the absolute most positive way!

~ Diane, Camden's mom; 33; Texas, United States

Blogging @ www.mycsinthecountry.blogspot.com

{Asher}

I am the mom of three boys. My second son was born with a birth defect called Spina bifida. It is a defect of the spine and can often be diagnosed via ultrasound while the baby is in utero. When we decided to have a third child we asked to have periodic ultrasounds so we could look

for any signs of Spina bifida. This was just so we knew how to proceed in plans for the birth. We were always sure we would have this baby.

At 20 weeks we had an ultrasound done by a perinatologist. At the appointment he told us there were no markers for Spina bifida and the baby looked to have a completely intact spine but there were several markers for Down syndrome. My heart felt so heavy I thought it might fall out of my chest. I had been so focused on Spina bifida I hadn't even thought of any other possibility. I was in shock. The doctor offered several different tests but they all had risks to the baby and we wanted the baby regardless of the results, so we refused them and went home.

Over the next weeks I felt in a panic. I talked to family and friends who had similar markers, a spot on the heart, enlarged kidneys, advanced maternal age, whose babies had turned out perfectly fine. My fears began to diminish. I was just sure God was not going to give us two babies with special needs.

At the 32 week recheck the spot on the heart had disappeared. So, with only the two other markers our odds of having a baby with Down syndrome went down significantly. Both my husband and I relaxed completely, sure that this meant the baby would be fine.

At exactly 38 weeks I went into labor. It was a fast labor. I had a planned homebirth. My midwives made it in time to guide the baby out, within 20 minutes of their arrival Asher Riley was there.

Right away the midwives knew something was not quite right. He never opened his eyes. He never cried. It was like he was sleeping, through the entire birthing process. The midwife started to do mouth to mouth on him hoping to perk him up and wake him. His color pinked up, he had been very blue, but still there was no sound and no eyes looking around.

We decided to transport to the hospital.

At the hospital we learned that Asher weighed in at 10 pounds, 2 ounces and was 22 inches long. We also learned he had many markers for Down syndrome. As soon as the pediatrician said we think he has Down syndrome the tears started falling. This was not supposed to happen again. I was not supposed to have another baby with special needs. I was supposed to be cuddling my new baby at home, on my bed, surrounded by my loving family, with my husband cooking me French toast in the kitchen! What kind of rotten joke was this?!

I remember at some point my husband whispering in my ear that he looked just like our first born and they must be mistaken. I remember grasping on to that last thread of hope, willing him to be right. The next two weeks Asher was in the NICU of our local Children's Hospital. He had to be tube fed for the first week and a half because he didn't want to wake up and do it himself. We were told of the test results, that Asher did indeed have Down syndrome.

I felt anxious, scared, angry at my body for 'messing up' again, angry at God for not fixing things. But the more I held my new baby, and smelled him, and touched him the more those negative feelings started to wash away. Asher didn't open his eyes for the first four days of life and the first time he looked at me I thought not just my heart but my entire body would melt from sheer joy.

Moments of joy just kept coming. Watching his older brothers with him was amazing. Their unconditional acceptance and love for him was a testimony to me. When my middle son whispered in his ear, 'It's okay, Asher. I'll protect you,' I realized that this was a great place to be. This was our normal. This was where I belonged. It may not look like what the world portrayed as the perfect, typical family but this place was incredible and so much more than that cookie cutter image!

I have learned through my second son and now with Asher that there will be moments of sorrow and grief, moments where I will wish things were different, where I will be sorrowful that things are so hard for Asher. And I must allow myself to embrace these times, allow myself to grieve. That is part of the process. But I also must force myself to let those moments go because if I hold on to them I will never get to experience the incredible gift it is to get to be Asher's mom.

And he really is a gift. Our family has been changed because of his existence. We are all better people because he is in our world.

~ Kristin, Asher's mom; 35; Minnesota, United States

Blogging @ http://countitalljoy.blogspot.com/

{Isabel}

In June of 2011, at ten weeks pregnant, I went in for an ultrasound and found out that our baby's heart was no longer beating. I was devastated. We had lost two babies prior to our oldest child and now a third? My husband Mike and I decided that we should be content with our two healthy daughters and made plans for him to get a vasectomy. We just couldn't bear the thought of losing another little one and going through that incredibly painful experience ever again.

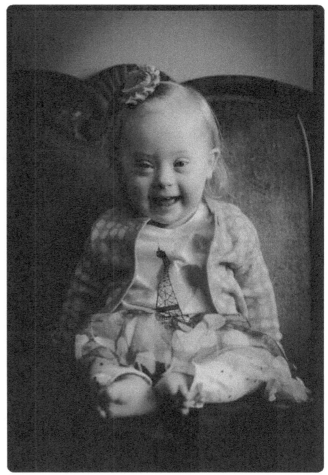

Despite our intentions, time passed and we never got around to scheduling Mike's procedure. It was December and I was extremely busy getting ready for the holidays. Our baby's due date had been December 24th and I couldn't help but feel sadness that the one Christmas gift I desperately wanted would not be arriving. A few days later I realized that my period was late and quickly ran to the store to get a pregnancy test. I took the test and two pink lines showed up and I couldn't help but feel joy where there once had been sadness. God was repairing my broken heart and giving us this unexpected chance to add another blessing to our family.

My pregnancy was fairly uneventful. I declined all genetic testing despite being considered at risk due to my "advanced maternal age" of 36 years old. I figured any major health problems would be apparent on our ultrasounds. We found out that we were having another girl and decided to name her Isabel.

My c-section was scheduled and on August 17th, 2012, we headed to the hospital to meet this new little one. Isabel arrived much like her sisters, getting pulled out of me, cold and crying. I was relieved at the sound and couldn't help but cry my own tears of thankfulness that she appeared to be healthy. I impatiently waited to get a close look at our new daughter. It felt like an eternity but when they finally brought her to me, I immediately noticed that she looked quite a bit different from our other daughters and for a moment I felt a tinge of worry. I quickly brushed it off as nothing and relaxed while they whisked her off to our recovery room with Mike.

While they were sewing me up, Mike had some time to get a further look at our new arrival. He couldn't help but notice that her neck looked a little different in addition to her facial features. Although neither of us had any experience with Down syndrome, he immediately felt that these features pointed in that direction. He wasted no time in expressing these concerns to our nurse, who quickly dismissed his questions as silly. When I arrived in the room, the nurse finished cleaning Isabel up and handed her to Mike so she could get me situated in our new room. It was then that Mike asked for a third time if she may have Down syndrome. After an uncomfortable period of silence, our nurse quietly approached us and told us her suspicions that our baby did in fact have Down syndrome. In that instant it felt like the world had collapsed all around me. I felt numb as she showed us all of the physical markers that Isabel displayed. Our nurse went on to tell us that our little girl could have a hard time nursing due to something called "low tone".

Breastfeeding was something that was so important to me that I immediately felt a need to prove her wrong. Surprisingly, Isabel latched on beautifully and nursed like a pro. I felt comforted in this fact and rejoiced in Isabel's success.

Somehow Mike and I were able to hold it together in these first moments. There were no tears, no sadness and no anger. After we were transferred to our permanent room we knew it was time to allow our parents, siblings and girls in to meet our newest addition. Despite Isabel not being what we expected, I did not want there to be sadness. I also felt that the news should be relayed to our family before they came to the room. I knew I would break down in tears if I was the one to say something so I asked Mike to tell them in the waiting room. When our family finally entered our room, we received congratulations, love and joy over our new little one and for this I will be eternally grateful.

Our plan had been for Mike to return to our home with the girls for the night. I knew that, like me, he was hurting on the inside and desperately needed time to himself to process everything before we could talk together. Thankfully his parents agreed to watch the girls and he was able to have that alone time.

That night, while in my room with Isabel, I finally allowed myself to grieve for the child that was not to be. Desperate to talk to someone, I called my dear friend Val. Through my sobbing and tears I told her the news and shared my fears. My biggest fear was that I could not be the mother that Isabel needed. I could barely handle my two girls, how could I handle a child with special needs?

Despite my grief, I shared my belief that Isabel would be good for our family. I knew that she would shape us into better people. But would we be able to give HER the love and care that SHE needed? Adding to my fear was the very scary list of possible medical issues she could have that the pediatrician had shared with us earlier that afternoon. I poured my heart out to her and like always, she told me exactly what I needed to hear.

With our older girls with our parents, Mike and I spent the next two days in the hospital together with our new little girl. She seemed to be doing remarkably well. Despite this, we were fearful that Isabel could have a serious heart problem and our pediatrician arranged for her to get an Echocardiogram before we were discharged. Thankfully, there were no serious defects found and we were free to go home.

We couldn't go home without a middle name for our baby. Initially we had wanted her to be Isabel Sophia, but that just didn't seem right. Despite our concerns, we could already tell that she would bring happiness to our lives and there really wasn't any other middle name that could fit except "Joy".

After we arrived home, we struggled to get our little girl to stay awake and eat. Although she did well at breastfeeding, she continued to lose weight due to her sleepiness. I eventually started giving her pumped breast milk with added calories and finally she was able to gain weight. Isabel also had another Echocardiogram and thankfully that did not show any areas of concern.

When Isabel was six weeks old, we had our first meeting with the "Help Me Grow" Early Intervention Program. They thought she was doing great but were a little concerned with her vision as she had not started to track things. While we waited to see the Ophthalmologist, I almost convinced myself that she was blind. After a thorough eye exam, we found out that while she did have clogged ducts and nystagmus, Isabel's vision was completely fine.

These first two months were consumed with worry over immediate feeding concerns, therapy questions and uncertainty about her health. I spent a lot of time online researching feeding techniques, therapy, vision questions and learning as much as I could about life with Down syndrome. I bonded fiercely with Isabel. I also clung to God. I filled the room with praise music to help me stay awake during our night-time feeds but also to fill my spirit with hope.

We finally made it past survival mode when Isabel was 2 1/2 months old. We had gotten into a routine and she was growing and healthy. It was then that the diagnosis really hit me. I started to realize all of the ways that she was going to be "different" and I entered into a dark place. What eventually helped pull me out of my depression was the adorable

smiles I started to receive from our little girl. I also joined a Facebook group for moms of babies born around the same time frame that offered support and encouragement.

Isabel is about to turn one and is doing remarkably well. She is sitting up, pulling to stand and signing new words every day. She has been a healthy baby and our life is normal. As I reflect on our first year I am amazed at how much a little baby can affect change. I still feel inadequate as a mother, but I'm learning to give it all to God and let Him work in me. I will do everything I can to ensure Isabel is confident in her identity and knows that she is an awesome creation.

Although my period of depression was difficult, I think it was in my brokenness that I was able to let go of the plans that I had for my life and come to a place of acceptance. I had to come to terms with my ideas of what constitutes a meaningful life, what beauty really is and face the reality that we are now "that" family. Of course there are days that I still struggle, but I can see the good in this and see the gifts that she will give us... Patience, compassion, humility, kindness, joy and most of all, love.

~Heather, Isabel's mom; 36; Minnesota, United States

{James}

It seems fitting that our story began at the base of Hope Pass in Leadville. I didn't know it then, but that was the first week of my first pregnancy. It's a 3,000 foot climb filled with dreams and adventure, but also full of doubt and challenges. It is here that people's dreams soar and people's dream are crushed. I had no idea what it would mean for me to stand on top of that pass a year later and how different my life would be.

A few months later I was having a healthy pregnancy and received my quad screen results for Down syndrome which were 1in 8500. I knew there was still that slight possibility, but there were no other soft markers and it really didn't matter to me so I opted out of further testing. At 33

weeks, my baby was diagnosed with intrauterine growth restriction (IUGR). He was tiny, not growing and my placenta was failing. We decided to induce him at 37 weeks to give him the opportunity to grow better.

It was the scariest 41 hours of my life. James wasn't tolerating the induction well; his heart rate kept dropping really low. We would back off the pitocin, wait

Megan Newton PHOTOGRAPHY

for his heart rate to stabilize and start again. Finally my OB said we could try one more time, but it was time to start talking about a c-section, which I desperately wanted to avoid. I guess James didn't want a c-section either and he finally made his appearance into this world.

We had decided to be surprised by the gender and my husband was literally speechless when he saw our baby was a boy. What we didn't expect was we were about to get another surprise. James was my first so I didn't really know what to expect, but he was blue and not crying, so I was definitely worried. They got him on oxygen and I was finally able to hold him for about 30 seconds before they rushed him down to the NICU. About 30 minutes later the neonatologist walked back into my delivery room, sat down and said, "I have some bad news". All I could think was my tiny baby is in the NICU I don't know what's wrong with him, but apparently it's something pretty serious. I had just endured a long, stressful labor and I wasn't sure how much more I could handle. "He has Down syndrome," were the next words out of his mouth. I'm not sure what I had expected him to say, but this wasn't it.

I was a mix of emotions, not sure what to think or do. My mind raced as I ran through a list of possibilities, but I realized there was only one option. I was going to be the mom of a boy with Ds. I didn't know if I could do it, I didn't know what it meant and tears streamed down my face as I realized all of this.

My heart ached wondering what this new life would be like, wondering what had happened to the little child I had spent 8 months dreaming about. The runs we would go on, the mountain tops we would view the world from. Was any of this going to be possible? My heart still aches sometimes wondering if he will ever get to experience falling in love. To me this has been one of the hardest emotional hurdles. I know James may find the love of his life and fall madly in love, but he may not and that breaks my heart to think about.

I was so scared seeing him on the warming table in the NICU that a nurse had to tell me it was okay to touch him. I lightly touched his hand and he grabbed my finger fiercely as if begging me to let him know it was okay and that I still loved him. In that moment I knew not only would everything be okay, but everything would be better, not necessarily easier, but definitely better because James had now blessed my life. Tears welled up again.

James had a short NICU stay to help regulate his body temperature, stabilize his oxygen saturation, for jaundice and NG tube feeding. Within an hour of James being born they scoped his digestive system and performed an echocardiogram. We were told everything looked okay and we were encouraged that our little fighter was at least healthy.

We never got that moment where we left the delivery room and they played a lullaby through the hospital for James, I never got wheeled out the hospital with a little baby in my lap. I think that was one of the most heartbreaking things for me. Somehow I felt like our baby wasn't worth that picture perfect moment. But when we did get to break James out of the NICU it was so much better than the picture perfect dream I had imagined. We were taking our little boy home to be a family.

Once we got home we had to take James to his pediarician for weekly weight checks and oxygen saturation checks, he came home on oxygen due in part to us living at 9,000 feet in elevation. At his one month check-up his pediatrician noticed a heart murmur and asked about his echocardiogram. He asked me to wait while he called the cardiologist who reviewed his echo while we were in the NICU. He came back and explained James had two holes in his heart and we would need to see a cardiologist about a potential heart surgery. My own heart sank and it was all I could do not to break down crying. A couple days later we were at the Children's Hospital for the first time to meet our cardiologist. After his echo and chest x-ray he explained James had a PDA, ASD, VSD, pulmonary hypertension and pulmonary stenosis and would likely need open heart surgery by the time he was one. I was numb, no thoughts, no emotions, nothing. I was pretty sure I wasn't hearing this doctor correctly. He must have looked at the wrong results. We left being told we were waiting for James to go into heart failure. There were a lot of sleepless nights after that. When James was almost 4 months old he started the initial phases of heart failure. We started him on medication to clear the fluid from his lungs and continued to wait.

And then we got our Christmas miracle. Just before Christmas we went for a cardiology follow-up and were expecting to schedule heart surgery. But instead James no longer showed signs of heart failure. His cardiologist said we would continue to monitor him, but the chances of open heart surgery were now 50/50. As we have continued to monitor his VSD it has started to close and the chance of open heart surgery has decreased.

When we first took James to meet his pediatrician he told us "James is complicated and is going to scare us from time to time." He was right on.

Twenty-two months after bringing him home from the NICU he's still on supplemental oxygen. He has had multiple surgeries to: place ear tubes and eye stents, remove his adenoids, fix his epiglottis and heart and check his lungs. James' medical journey has been a wild ride; an endless stream of appointments, tests and trips to the Children's Hospital. There are days I just feel completely overwhelmed by it and there are days I just take it all in stride. I am grateful he hasn't had any major issues, but it's still frustrating that his little body is fighting all of these other things when other kids get to focus more on their therapy. I know the day will come when I'm just worried about James breaking an arm playing soccer, we just have a ways to go to get there…he's complicated.

James has a smile that melts heart, eyes that light up a room and a giggle that never leaves your heart. In the time I have had to get to know James he has taught me patience, acceptance, selflessness and hope. It's been a hard journey. There are days where I wonder how this is my life now. And there are days where I wonder how I got so lucky to have James as my son. I love my little guy so much, his eyes hold so much promise for his future, so much joy and love that I know I can handle this and I will. With each mile of trail I ran after he was born allowed me to work through and accept his Ds diagnosis and to deal with the medical issues that have come along with Ds. With James there have been hills, more ups and downs, and my unsure footings, but the most beautiful views are after the massive climb.

Three months after James was born I stood on top of Hope Pass for the first time. As I stood there, in the dark, I looked back at where I came from and ahead at the miles that lay before me and I smiled. I have stood in that same spot many times since, always with a smile and always remembering the journey that has led me there.

~Siobhan; James' mom; 33; Colorado, United States

Blogging @ www.co-running.blogspot.com

{Jasmine}

We had everything planned. My husband and I planned to have two kids close in age and we were blessed to conceive both times in my first cycle. My older daughter was just six months old when I got pregnant of our second baby. My doctor had alerted me about the risks of Autism with my pregnancies being so close together but I was certain my baby would be born perfectly healthy. Besides my aches and pains, I had an uneventful pregnancy. All tests and ultrasounds were okay and my doctor even joked that I was in "cruise control". I was not too worried about the baby's health when I went to the hospital on February 18, 2013 for a scheduled c-section. Baby seemed healthy, had 10 toes, 10 fingers and she was in breech position.

At 39w and 3 days, our baby Jasmine was born measuring 8lbs 3oz and 20.5 inches. Right after the surgery she was brought to my arms. She seemed perfect, she was beautiful. They brought her to me, we did skin to skin, I fed her and they wheeled us into our room where my parents and my in laws anxiously waited for us. It was a real birthday party! We took lots of pictures, sipped on champagne and even had Surf and Turf for dinner. A real treat at my hospital for the new parents!!

That night, after everyone had left the hospital, my husband was sleeping in the couch, baby was in the bassinet, I had nurses coming in and out of the room and for some reason I felt alone, I felt alone like never before. It was 3am...I was awake and worried of what I was seeing in my Jasmine's sweet little face. I could not help but wonder, did they see it too? Up to that point, no doctors or nurses had mentioned Down syndrome to us. Baby was over 12 hrs old when I started crying compulsively and woke up my husband. I was in shock; I could not believe my eyes or my thoughts. I could not share my worries with my husband. It was almost as if I said them out loud, they somehow would become real. I had spent the last few hours holding my baby in one hand and searching the Internet with the other hand. I had checked my baby's delicate body for all Down syndrome's marks: she certainly had the almond shaped eyes, the flat small nose, the small ears, rounded face, flat profile but she was still so much alike my older daughter. She was beautiful, just perfect! She did not have the single crease across her palms, the short stubby fingers, and the larger gap between her toes, nor any apparent heart condition. When I finally calmed myself down and was strong enough to first say out loud the two words 'Down syndrome', my husband's first reaction was to deny it. He had not noticed her almond shaped eyes nor suspected anything wrong with our perfect baby girl. He hugged me and let me cry for a very long time. I don't think I ever cried so much in my entire life. Since the beginning he has always assured me things would be fine and that he would always be the best husband and father he could be.

Next morning, when the pediatrician came to exam our baby for the first time, I could not wait to ask her about my suspicious diagnosis. She mentioned about Jasmine's low muscle tone and almond shaped eyes, but she was not very sure of the diagnosis. That same day, I could not stop wondering how we did not find that out during our pregnancy. I thought all the tests indicated a normal baby. I was devastated. I was pissed at my OBGYN. I had trusted him. Why did my baby have Down syndrome? Before getting pregnant my husband and I had talked about a possible termination if we were to find out our baby had any disability. We had no choice. Jasmine was here, she was in my arms, she was perfect and needed our love.

The next morning, right before we left the hospital the nurses collected her blood sample and I was told the genetics results would take about 2-3 weeks. Two entire weeks? How would I survive the unknown for two entire weeks? I wanted to stay at the hospital and run all sorts of tests on her, but the doctors said she had a clean bill of health and was ready to go home. She did not have any medical issues common with kids with Down syndrome, no heart defect, no vision or hearing problems, no thyroid issues.

We decided to write a letter to inform our friends of her syndrome even before receiving the official diagnosis, I could not imagine having to tell and explain all of my friends and family in person that she was not perfect, that she has an extra chromosome. All I did for the first two weeks was cry. I read many blogs, books; so much was going through my mind. I was afraid I would lose my friends; that they would slowly distance themselves from us. I am glad I was wrong, they have been really supportive. Most people were surprised like we were at first, but everyone said we had been blessed and that God gives his harder battles to his strongest soldiers. I joined several local and online support groups. I started going to church again, started counselling and have created a great support team.

In the first 36 hours of life, there was a whirlwind of emotions and I was completely overwhelmed. I had no idea what the future would hold, and I was scared to death. While there is still not a day that I do not worry about the future, I can honestly say that our journey has been much more enjoyable than I could have ever imagined. Jasmine is a wonderful baby and I pray that our future together continues to be surprisingly normal. I was, and still am, worried about her differences, but the unconditional love for her I have in my heart is still unbelievable.

~ Juliana, Jasmine's mom; 32; Florida, United States

On Facebook @
https://www.facebook.com/PrincessJasmineSchallert)

{Lilly}

One night I had a dream where a man told me I was pregnant. We had been trying to conceive for 5 months. I felt suddenly excited and knew I had to take a pregnancy test. However, it was a work day. I was meeting my first client at the local shopping mall at 9:30am. Before our appointment I quickly purchased a test and waited anxiously for my client to arrive. Much to my delight she didn't appear, so in a public toilet of our local Westfield Shopping Centre I found my self staring back and forth at the results, "Am I reading this right, could I really be pregnant?"

I called in sick for work and went straight to the local medical centre for confirmation. The results were positive and I was feeling really nervous about telling my husband. He had wanted to wait a while to have children but had agreed to start trying, as he thought this would lower the chances of a disability. He was happy with the news in a calm, male sort of way. I however, was over the moon. We were offered the blood test to check for trisomy 21 at 8 weeks but declined for two reasons. Firstly, abortion was not an option for us and secondly, we didn't think we

would have a child with Down syndrome; after all I was only 27 and healthy. However, at my 20 week scan things were about to get very real. My ultrasound lasted for 3 hours and I was contacted the next day by my GP asking me if I could go straight to the hospital as there were some abnormalities presenting on the scan. I burst into tears and fear started to flood my body. I had no idea what to expect. However, there was a part of me that always knew something wouldn't be "quite right".

As a Christian I spend time praying and reading my Bible. Just before I became pregnant I felt directed to read a passage in Matthew 6. This section talks about not worrying and seeking God first and he will meet our needs. One part of the scripture says;

"Consider the lilies of the field, how they grow: they neither toil nor spin; [29] and yet I say to you that even Solomon in all his glory was not arrayed like one of these."

I felt God saying, "Do not worry, Lilly is going to be okay," We had decided to not find out the sex of our child but I had a strong feeling I was going to have a daughter and if this was so I was to call her Lilly. A friend had also contacted me before I knew I was pregnant saying she had a dream that I was going to have a baby and she was to pray for me throughout my pregnancy.

When I was summoned to the hospital it didn't come as a shock but I did feel very apprehensive. The doctor told us that our baby didn't have a nasal bone, she had an echogenic bowl and her spine seemed to be fused incorrectly. We were told she could have cystic fibrosis, spina bifida, Down syndrome or none of the above. We were sadly offered an abortion (which we declined straight away), and where also asked if we would like some further testing. My husband and I took some time to think and decided not to get any further tests and asked the doctors not to mention it anymore.

I felt confident that everything would be okay. After all why would God tell me not to worry, that I am having a girl, give me her name and guide my friend to pray for me? I went through the rest of my pregnancy praying daily and honestly believing that my baby would be born "normal." In hindsight I can see the message 'not to worry' was not only for the 38 weeks and 4 days of my pregnancy but for Lilly's whole life.

On the 5.4.13 I was admitted to hospital at 38 weeks and 3 days. My baby was small, the fluid around her was almost nonexistent and there were concerns the placenta had stopped feeding her. I was induced and after a 5 hour labours on 6.4.13 my darling Lilly Grace was born and lifted onto my chest. Filled with happiness and awe I held my perfect, alive, crying baby girl. Shortly after her birth the paediatrician examined Lilly. When they gave her back to me they said they were pretty sure she has Down syndrome but they would need to send off the placenta for confirmation. It felt like I had a huge hole in my stomach and grief and sickness began to consume me. I remained in hospital for over a week as Lilly had difficulty feeding. Through out my stay all the midwives were speaking about Lilly as if the diagnosis had already been confirmed. They were very kind, however, I wasn't ready to come on board with Lilly's diagnosis.

The two weeks before we got the official results were like a rollercoaster but not a fun one at a theme park. This was like a roller coaster through a grave yard, with zombies chasing you trying to take your life. It was very, very scary, "My daughter can't have Down syndrome I'm only 27."

"That kind of thing only happens to other people. Does this mean my chances are higher if I was to have other children?" My hormones mixed together with   grief and fear, left me feeling confused and overwhelmed.

When I arrived home I received a pack from the Down syndrome association. I began reading a book called "Parents guide to raising a child with Down syndrome". This book was quickly

discarded when I came to the section about all the possible sickness. I spent time in prayer and felt God direct me back to the scripture. "Consider the lilies of the field, how they grow". I felt him say again "Don't worry, Lilly will be fine". I decided to discard all negativity and stop dwelling on the 'what ifs'. My daughter is 3 months old and first smiled when she was 6 weeks old. She now lifts her head when lying on her stomach, is starting to grasp and play with her toys, sucks her thumb and rolls to her side and just started to roll onto her stomach.

I see it as a blessing that I didn't know about Lilly's diagnosis prenatally. If I had known, I would have prepared for Down syndrome. Instead, I prepared for Lilly. I prepared for a child, a family, a gift – not a syndrome. My baby girl is such a gift.

My passion now is to see many more children like my daughter given the opportunity for life. I believe it's not our right to choose to take life away. That is God's choice and his alone. Had I chosen to abort my baby I would have been destroying a beautiful little girl who deserves the chance to life just like you and me.

The bible says in Psalm 139:13-16

"For you created my inmost being;

  you knit me together in my mother's womb.

[14] I praise you because I am fearfully and wonderfully made;

  your works are wonderful,

  I know that full well.

[15] My frame was not hidden from you

  when I was made in the secret place,

  when I was woven together in the depths of the earth.

[16] Your eyes saw my unformed body;

  all the days ordained for me were written in your book

  before one of them came to be."

God designed and created my baby girl, God breathed life into her and I am very thankful and happy.

~Katrina, Lilly's mum; 27; Australia

{Elijah}

Elijah came three weeks early, born at 37 weeks 1 day. I was driving back from my weekly check-up at my doctors when somebody pulled out in front of me and I had to slam my brakes on. Thankfully I have ABS (anti-lock breaking system) so didn't hit them, but it set contractions off. Around an hour later I was calling an ambulance to take me to hospital! I honestly doubted I was going to make it in time.

Elijah was born within an hour of arriving. Straight away I knew something wasn't right as he looked like he was crying but there was no sound and he was very purple. I kept babbling about it but they rushed him straight out for oxygen all the time telling me he was ok. They then came back in and told me he was in NICU (neonatal intensive care unit).

A midwife rushed in with excitement at one point going on about his abnormalities - short fingers, his face - and I had no idea what she was on about!! I still don't understand why she was so upbeat about it either.

Elijah was born on June 12th 2012, weighing 3602g. It was three very long hours before I was able to see him. He was in a humidicrib with a CPAP machine (oxygen) and I was only allowed to touch him.

At 24 hours old, he was wheeled in for surgery for an imperforate anus. After surgery late in the afternoon I was able to go and see how my little man was going in NICU. While I was down there with my mum they broke the news about his diagnosis... He has Down syndrome. I don't remember a lot of what the diagnosing neonatologist, Dr C, was saying and I teared up, but was trying so hard to be strong. What never left me was Dr C talking about testing in pregnancy and I told him straight I wouldn't go through with it and wouldn't trust the results. His response was, "Really?" in a condescending tone.

When I left NICU I went outside to ring those close to me and tell them and broke down. I remember a stranger walking by and asking if I was okay; she was really worried to leave me there crying. I admit I was naive at this stage. I didn't have much idea about Down syndrome at all; and certainly not how it would, or could, affect his life – our life. I've since found out my thoughts were normal but I worried I wouldn't be able to continue study, wouldn't be able to work in the future, what was his future going to be, what was mine, schooling; the list goes on... I also worried if something were to happen to him would I be blamed. I've been told it's a grieving process of sorts. I had already lost my husband, though newly separated at the time, to suicide and another lady I know pass from breast cancer. And here I was being told I would go through a grieving process for the third time in less than 12 months. And grieve I did... for the 'ideal' baby I thought I was going to have.

But, you know what? How wrong I was!! He is perfect, and special, just the way he is. I can study. I can work if I choose to. His future is bright. Sure we'll have people look at him differently, it's how we deal with it and raise him that will make all the difference. A few days after diagnosis I decided "I WANT TO REBEL AGAINST CONFORMITY"... If people are going to judge my little boy, they'll have to judge his mum too. So eventually I did colour my hair, shaved some of it, and that's the way it's staying :) It's actually quite liberating!!

Elijah is 14 months old. He's now started the bridge pose and we are working on walking. The physio is so impressed with his strength we aren't 'focussing' on anything at the moment. I have started simple signs with him and he has his ENT surgery this week, otherwise healthy. Adored by all our family & his sisters can't leave him alone. Even on my darkest of days, just seeing him smile brightens my day; he's brought us so much joy & inspiration.
I'll finish this post with a quote from my friend. "It's like the kids song "going on a bear hunt". You can't go over it, you can't go under it, you can't go round it, you've got to go THROUGH it."

~Kat, Elijah's mum; 32; Australia

{Ari}

Several hours after the lovely water birth of our son, Ari, our nurse took him to the end of the bed to take his measurements. Everyone seemed very quiet and I assumed it was just because it was early in the morning after a long night.

I remember everyone leaving my room and then our midwife and nurse returning and telling us they needed to go over some things. Our Midwife began by saying that they had found some things while doing Ari's checkup. He had low ears, short fingers, a gap between his toes, single palmer creases on his hands. I listened in a daze, wishing she would get to the point, not having a clue what that point might be. Before she got to it, Tim interrupted and said, "does he have Down syndrome? I was shocked to hear him say it, like he had been suspecting it all along. I found out later he had thought his eyes looked

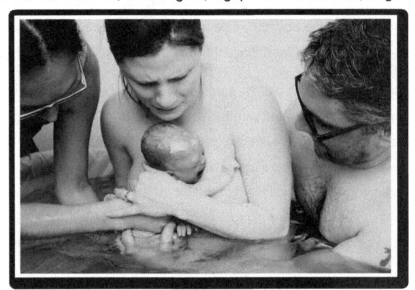

funny and had gone to the restroom and googled images of babies with Down syndrome. I couldn't see anything different in him, so I was taken off guard. Laura answered by telling us that she can't tell us if he does have Down syndrome, and only a genetic test could confirm that, but that the markers they found all point to this being the case. Both her and Melissa cried and tried to comfort us by telling us that he was going to be the most loving and wonderful child. They told us that we need to be transferred to the hospital to check his heart and that an ambulance would come to transport him. I don't remember crying, just staring into nothingness and feeling completely numb except for the burning knot in my gut. The ladies left the room and shut the door and Tim and I hugged and cried. I remember very clearly that all he said to me through his tears was, "I love you so much."

The ENT's entered with a cart to take Ari out in. Tim and I were to drive over separately while Ari went in the ambulance. I remember someone saying how handsome Ari was and I feigned a smile and didn't go to him before he was wheeled away. I didn't recognize him as mine at that moment and it felt so awful.

We were directed to Ari's room in the NICU and I was propped up in a chair by one of the nurses, who handed me my boy, hooked up to a million wires. She helped tuck him inside my shirt to warm up and told Tim and I to try to get some rest. She turned off the lights and closed the door. I remember closing my eyes and leaning back in the chair, willing myself to sleep. I was convinced that when I woke up, this nightmare would be over, and I could go back to the time before he was born. Eventually they found a room for us to sleep in and we decided to leave Ari for a short bit to try to rest. Tim wheeled me to our room and we each took a hospital bed and curled up in balls. I began to fall into sleep, but Tim was sobbing and I couldn't sleep without trying to comfort him first. I curled up behind him and we cried hard together. He told me that he did "not want this." He didn't want to be a "special needs parent." I said I didn't either, but what could we do? He told me his heart was broken and it broke me to hear that. I had thoughts in that room, thoughts I don't like to admit. We felt at times that our life was over. But I told myself that he was my baby and I loved him, even if it felt like he wasn't mine, or at

least he wasn't the baby I had expected. I told Tim that he was just a baby and he needed his parents. All we could do was be there for him and love him.

I believe the grieving was a very necessary part of our experience and inevitably led to healing. We got the final word on his genetic test results, and though we were expecting it, it was still hard to hear.

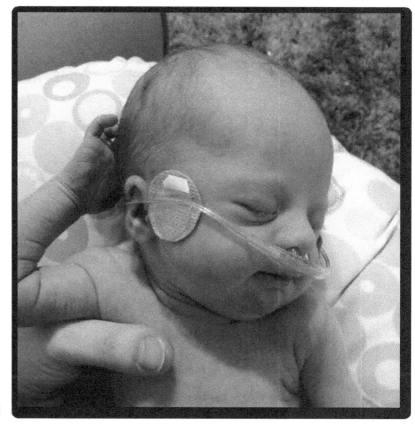

One of the first mornings I recall, I was holding Ari after a feeding and in the NICU room alone with him. I sang to him and cried. I whispered to him that I was sorry. I was so so sorry that I couldn't give him a better life.

Several weeks later, once we had been home for awhile, I sat on our bed holding Ari and I started on again about how sorry I was and that he wasn't going to have a very good life, when it hit me – he was going to love his life! And we were going to give him every opportunity. He may not have the exact life that was in our heads, but it wasn't about us anymore. It was about him and his happiness. 99% of adults with Down syndrome report being happy with their lives. I can't imagine that number would be anywhere near as high in the general population. This was just the beginning of my acceptance of our situation and the rest of our story is still unfolding. What I can say right now is that I couldn't love my son more if I tried. He brings me joy tenfold and brightens my days. I truly believe that he will do great things in his life.

Ari is almost 18 months now and is doing amazingly well! We haven't had any additional health issues. He is taking steps and so close to walking! He keeps us entertained all day because he is so silly. We are constantly in awe of just how smart he is. He understands so much more than we might give him credit for. He is following commands and signing about 10 words. We truly couldn't be more proud of him or love him any more than we do!

~ Lacey, Ari's mom; 27; Colorado, United States

Blogging @ http://youmightgetlost.blogspot.com/

{Alaina}

I knew all along – good ol' mother's intuition I guess. I think friends and family got tired of me saying over and over again, "I just want the baby to be healthy." I remember sitting on my husband's lap in our office, after getting out of the hospital for pre term contractions, looking at the 3-D ultrasounds photo of our baby's face. "Squirt (what we lovingly nicknamed the baby since we didn't know the gender) looks different – like it has Down syndrome." Where did those words come from?? I didn't even know anyone with Down syndrome…why would I say that? I knew. I had such anxiety about having her. Not about becoming a first time parent, but the actual birth…I knew something was not going to be right.

When I went to my last doctor's appointment at 36 ½ weeks and he told me I could go off the pills that were keeping my contractions at bay, all I could think about was the date of the following day and I thought…any day but that day, it holds so many sad memories. September 11th. But inside I knew it would happen.

I woke up in the middle of the night not feeling well. By 5 am, I knew I needed to get Bryan up. We called the hospital and were on our way. I said we'd see how I handled pain before I said yes to the epidural. Apparently I don't do pain well! I asked for it by the time we got to a room. I wasn't even 5 cm dilated yet, but I couldn't relax through the contractions. I think I dilated fully with half an hour after receiving the epidural! I pushed for 2 hours and at 9:25am, Thursday, September 11th, 2008, our 6 pound 12 ounce Alaina Marie entered the world. I had no idea what to expect. She came out crying like any baby should. It so ironic to me that I said those words about her ultrasound picture just three weeks prior, because when I looked at her, I didn't notice anything. The only thing I thought looked different were her ears, but our doctor even made mention that it was probably because she was early – I don't know if he knew and just didn't want to say anything at that moment or what. We did all the normal newborn things with her. We called family and spread the news that she was here. It was a couple hours later, our doctor came in the room and told us both he had a suspicion that Alaina may have Down syndrome, but he wasn't sure. She had some of the markers, but not all. So that left us feeling - should we worry or not? They would take a blood sample and send off for testing. The results could take weeks to receive. I'm not even sure what I was feeling at that moment in time. Shock maybe? Uncertainty? Yes. I can't say I was really scared or worried…I didn't know what to think. The doctor didn't seem certain – why should we jump to conclusions and worry if we didn't have to? We didn't tell our families of his suspicions.

By the next day, she was having a little trouble with her sat levels and keeping her temperature up. So she was spending a lot of time in the nursery. I still didn't know what to think at this point – I think I just wanted it to not be true, and it would probably turn out okay. I worry over nothing sometimes. I was sitting in my room talking with my parents when our doctor stopped by. I quietly asked if they had any results from the test yet. He said no, but at that point he told me it was a test just to confirm the diagnosis. He said she has Down syndrome. That was my turning point. After he left the room, I sat on the bed speechless. I lost it. My parents didn't know what to think. They had looked at her in the nursery just minutes before and had no suspicions, so they were shocked at my tears. I told them the news. From there on out, it became real. She had had some feeding issues, so we were finger feeding, she was jaundice and still having some temperature and oxygen level issues. Nothing major, but just not the first time parent experience one imagines in their mind. She had an EKG of her heart, which revealed a bicuspid aortic value and a small ASD, but nothing that was causing her any medical issues and didn't cause her any from that point forward. We were so blessed with her good health.

We were in the hospital with her for six days. I remember the fear most. Fear of the unknown. All I knew were stereotypes. All I could do was replay my pregnancy in my mind, questioning everything I did. What did I do wrong? I didn't understand how it really worked and I didn't want to. I felt like I had let my husband down, everyone down – I didn't produce this perfect, healthy baby. I felt a sense of paranoia. Were people disappointed in me? Feel bad for us? I felt like they were always looking at me to see if I was holding it together....I was the only one I really saw cry - everyone else seemed to be able to hold it all together, or they just accepted it much better than I did. I felt such guilt. I know others had the same feelings as me, sometimes I wish someone could have said, "Forget being strong" and just cried it out with me. What happened to that baby I had carried for nine months? The one I was expecting to have? Where did that baby go? There was grieving. Telling people was hard. Everyone wanted to be positive and say the right things. I felt like I couldn't be sad. I had a healthy baby (she really was healthy compared to issues we could have faced) and everyone was saying how grateful I should be. But I didn't feel that way. I loved her because she was my child, but I didn't feel that mother-newborn connection you always hear women talk about. I didn't know her – especially this baby that I wasn't expecting. Then you feel the guilt on top of it all for feeling like you're not in love with your child the way you are supposed to be.

The nurses were wonderful. We live in a rural area, so our hospital was relatively small – sometimes you are the only patient in the hospital. We got some amazing, personalized care. One nurse went to town printing off article after article about Down syndrome and put it all in a black 3-ring binder. I couldn't bring myself to open it. It was enough to just do the day to day things. I didn't want to read about everything we could be facing raising her. It was too scary at the time. I never did open that binder. I put on blinders to so much those first few months. Being a new mom was enough – I couldn't face the what-if's.

There were lots of tears. I had more tears and fear then I care to admit looking back, but at the time that's how I felt, and a process I guess I had to take. But we took care of her and loved her like you should and things slowly changed over time. I still have hard days, I wouldn't want to go back and tell myself then to not cry or not be scared, but I wish I could have gone back and told myself about all the smiles, laughter and normality we would have too. Things that my naïve self didn't think was going to be possible.

So here we were at home…with a brand new baby and a whole different normal than we were even expecting. Alaina was 2 months old when the "Birth to 2" program came to visit the house for the first time. What a nerve-wracking event that felt like at the time. I already had this feeling of failure, now someone wanted to come "evaluate" my baby. Of course it was always worse in my mind than in real life! Little did I know how important those people would become to us – like family.

For three years, they came into our home every week for an hour and got to know Alaina – and me too. They were my sounding board, my reassurance, my information source. They were invaluable for Alaina's sake - and mine. The first few months I kind of coasted. I thought it was better for me to stay home. I didn't want Alaina to get sick, and honestly, it was hard to connect with others at that time. We had so many friends who were pregnant at the same time as us – it was like a club or something! And hearing of all their births, seeing their babies, hurt more than I could have imagined. We shared the same dream, shared pregnancy stories, shared congratulations…but our story ended much differently. While they were showing off their baby to family and friends and getting into a routine and thinking about going back to work, I was doing lots of the same things, but included were evaluations, cardiology visits, blood draws…things that didn't seem to be on any other parent's radars. I felt so different being in the same situation with someone else as I could possibly be. Yet looking back, things were obviously more normal than I realized. We did all the baby stuff everyone else did. It just felt so incredibly different at the time. But we were finally getting to "know" her. She loved her daddy – and still does. She was a super smiler and seemed to capture attention where ever we went – it was impossible not to. Once she learned how to wave, you were hard pressed to get by her without a wave and a smile! Besides being a big spitter, she was a pretty good baby. Best sleeper out of our three kids – so that's puts her in a little extra special place in our hearts, too! ☺

When Alaina was 6 months old, I got pregnant with our second child. I don't think anything more terrifying could have happened. I was excited, but scared you-know-what-less! Pregnancy no longer sounded enjoyable and exciting…it sounded like 9 months of worry. And it was – right or wrong. Everything was deemed normal for my first pregnancy and look what happened… If everything was "normal" for this pregnancy too, what kind of peace of mind does that give me? There was no peace of mind until Aubrey was born – I'm embarrassed to admit I couldn't look at her when she was born. I just told Bryan "just tell me she's ok….I can't look until I know she's ok." Our doctor was such a kind, wonderful man and had been with us since the beginning…he came into the room hours after Aubrey was born and I was alone and sat on the bed beside me and told me how proud he was of me – as he knew that day would be hard for me. If I wasn't already, that endeared me to him forever. He will probably never know how much those words meant to me and still bring me to tears to this day.

By the time Aubrey was born, we had settled into a good routine with Alaina. She had met so many of her milestones – sitting up at 6 months, crawling at 11 months and was cruising along furniture and walking behind push toys by the time she was 15 months. She nicely transitioned to eating table food and seemed to have no aversion to any of it. She had tubes in her ears when she was 9 months old and a week after, she started babbling up a storm and never really quit! I remember the first word we could distinguish for her was "ba-pa" (backpack on Dora! Kids aren't supposed to watch TV, right?? I could care less if it got her to talk!) It was true….life didn't seem as different as I feared it would. One of the big differences for me was the schedule of therapy. We started doing physical therapy with her before Aubrey was born, so we had occupational therapy, time with her early childhood special educator every week, and physical therapy every other week. Not to mention well baby visits, cardiologist checkups, ENT appointments and trips to specialized pediatricians who could give us evaluations and make suggestions on therapy for her. It felt like a full time job just keeping appointments straight and working around them sometimes. At that point, we were so thrilled with her progress and she was a bundle of personality that still attracted lots of attention and we were so proud.

I remember still feeling sadness some days – especially when we would get together with friends who had babies around the same time. It still kind of stung. Even though she wasn't at all, or at least not far behind those babies, discussions seemed odd. While they were talking

about what their kids were doing, just like I was, the rest of the conversation was filled with our therapy schedule and what she was working on or needed to try to work on…it's those things that made everything still feel different and brought sadness sometimes.

There were some wonderful mothers in the area who had kids with Down syndrome that reached out to me. I tried getting together with them a few times, and not because of anything they did at all, it wasn't working for me. It should have been a good support system, but it was hard to see the things their kids struggled with – it made me panic that Alaina would struggle with the same thing at some

point – which there was no validity to that thought at all. At the time it seemed very valid though. It wasn't my time to join these groups yet. As she has gotten older, it's gotten much easier for me and I've come to very much appreciate their support, insight and experience. A heartfelt, "I understand" goes a long way when you've hit a rough spot and are frustrated. And, "That's wonderful – way to go Alaina" at her accomplishments is so appreciated! They were a tremendous support when we had issues with services in our school district, too. Their encouragement and support meant a lot during that time.

As Alaina has gotten older, some things have gotten easier and some things have gotten more difficult. I'm not going to deny that I still cry, still have sad, hard days and still have so many questions – some days I almost feel no different than I did almost 5 years ago in terms of knowing the best way to help my daughter. I bring up the sad days so often because I do want mothers to know that it's okay to have sad days – no matter what age your kiddo is. Doesn't mean we don't love them to pieces, it means we're human. We love our kids fiercely and sometimes that means we feel their challenges and struggles, too. And I think that will always hurt for a mother.

Easier is the medical schedule…as we were blessed with her amazing health. Cardiology appointments have been stretched out to every 2 years, we don't see the specialized pediatricians anymore. We just go to the doctor when she's sick or for yearly check-ups. But therapy still remains a constant. We run more than we have to, and that's by my choosing. Any time someone can give us a different perspective or different activities to do with her, I'm all over it. I seek input from anyone who will give it to me. She's going into her third year at school – which she LOVES – and gets her weekly services there. But we also do additional physical and speech therapy at children's therapy clinic that's over an hour away. This summer we started hippotherapy with her, too. She rarely fights therapy – she so interactive and loves to play that she does pretty well – that doesn't mean that stubborn side doesn't ever come out though! ☺ And a stubborn side she can have – believe me! Now, my worries come more from thinking about her life long-term. What skills can we help her build and achieve to give her the best chance possible of having an independent and fulfilling life-however that may look for her? We still work on specific skills – cutting, writing, etc – but now we have lots of social skills to throw in the mix. The kids she goes to school with seem to adore her – which makes my heart happy. But I worry about her building friendships, being able to navigate social situations and helping her integrate into her classroom and peers as best we can.

But just like when she was first born, some days it seems so unnatural –our schedule. Spending so much time in therapy and driving to and from therapy. It consumes enough of our weekly routine that sometimes I don't feel like doing other things. Mommy guilt is tough as I feel like I neglect my other two kids to do all these activities with Alaina. But her brother and sister love her so. Their relationship is so heartwarming – to see Down syndrome through a child's eye is to not see it at all. They just see Alaina – wish it was that way to the whole world. She is one of the biggest bright spots in our family. Her smile, laugh and upbeat attitude is contagious. We couldn't be prouder of her hard work and all she has accomplished. It is true that every milestone seems so precious and is so celebrated. And we do lots of high fives and celebrating around here!

~Lauren, Alaina's mom; 29; Minnesota, United States

{Liam}

I had nine miscarriages before I finally got pregnant with our third child. I was under the care of a specialist at our hospital and had been for 2 years. From the earliest days of my pregnancy I was monitored and scanned, each ultrasound filled me with a sense of dread, but also excitement – wanting to see a heartbeat, but daring not to hope. I had opted to have the 12 week nuchal translucency scan, despite my fears, because it was another opportunity to make sure my baby was alive. I went alone and as soon as the sonographer placed the hand piece over my belly I could see the little heart beating away – pure relief! The scan went without a

hitch, it took a little longer, but everything looked great. At the end of the appointment I was told that they needed to speak to someone senior and asked me to wait in "the room".

My heart instantly sank. Something must be badly wrong because no one went into that room for good news. Alone, tears sprang to my eyes and the panic set in. It seemed like forever before someone came back and told me that, because it was now after hours, there were no senior staff available and I needed to go downstairs

straight away to speak to a doctor in women's assessment. I was led to an empty room, my legs practically crumbling from fear and two doctors sat down and told me that the scan had shown my baby had a 'slightly increased nuchal fold'. That, plus my age (42), meant my child was a high risk for Down syndrome. I fell to pieces in the chair. I was immediately offered a CVS the next day or told I could wait and have an amniocentesis a couple of weeks later to give a definite diagnosis. The female doctor was very reassuring, but I found myself asking if I would be forever judged by the medical fraternity if there was indeed something wrong with my baby and I had refused the testing. The pressure to test felt great, but for me, the risk of miscarrying this very much wanted baby was too high and the 1:200 risk of losing it meant there was no way I could agree. I suddenly felt trapped and needed to get out of there. We agreed that they would continue to monitor the pregnancy closely and use ultrasound to determine if there was indeed anything further to worry about.

I'm not sure how I drove home from the hospital, I was in no state to drive. When I got home I Googled 'Down syndrome' on my computer. Through the blur of my tears, lots of stereotypical images shot back at me, making me cry even more. I eventually stumbled on a blog about someone's child with Down syndrome and, as I read, I realised it was kind of positive. The more I read, the more I thought that maybe this wouldn't be the end of the world. My actual words to my husband that night were, "After reading that, I will almost be disappointed if this baby doesn't have DS!"

We talked a lot that night about how there are no guarantees in life, that our other two typical children could be struck down at any point and life could change. I relaxed as my husband spoke because I knew *I* could handle whatever we would be given, but I didn't know about him. It was reassuring to hear he was on the same page.

Our morphology ultrasound at 18 weeks was uneventful. The sonographer searched long and hard for 'soft' markers for Down syndrome, but there were none. I breathed a sigh of relief and we were overjoyed to find out we were having a boy!

At 20 weeks, I took the first photo of my pregnant belly and finally acknowledged that we were having a baby. There were more growth scans and a review at 32 weeks to check on a low lying placenta. It was at this scan that the sonographer brought me to tears when he flicked a button and there was a 3d image of my baby's face! He took some photos for me to take home and I proudly shared them with everyone. At my next antenatal appointment I showed my specialist the amazing pictures of our boy. Her words to me, "Well, he definitely doesn't have Down syndrome!"

The next five weeks were exciting. I felt pretty relaxed, despite still being scared of losing him. I was really starting to think that this dream was going to come true! It would take his birth to bring the world crashing down again. We could see it straight away. Our baby had Down syndrome.

Liam was born via planned caesarean section, due to my history of previous sections and being an insulin dependant diabetic, and as soon as he was delivered there was a silence in the air. In the photo taken as he was lifted out of me, you can see the two doctors looking at each other with frowns. When I held Liam I started asking straight away if he had Down syndrome. No-one replied. I asked my husband what he thought and he agreed with me. I asked my student midwife friend and she said the paediatrician would have to have a look. Despite the resolute silence, I was still filled with an overwhelming sense of joy at the birth of a live baby, nothing else mattered. At this point I didn't realise my husband wasn't coping. While I was in recovery our boy was taken to see the paediatrician on call who agreed that Down syndrome was evident from the physical features that presented themselves – epicanthal folds to eyes, low set ears and sandal gap between toes. The official results from genetic testing confirmed the rarer diagnosis of Mosaic Down syndrome two weeks later.

The news was conveyed to me that Liam's DS had been confirmed, but I seemed to be oblivious to everything else in my little bubble of happiness. Liam looked amazing to me! Back in my room, there was excitement as my parents and older two children came to join us. My husband however sat in the corner of the room, stony faced, silent and with his arms folded as if he was about to explode with rage. I have one photo of my husband holding his new son during the first two weeks of his life and it was taken at this moment when the midwife made him hold Liam while she checked my wound. My daughter took it, I remember her saying, 'Come on dad, smile'. It was painful and the tension in the room was palpable and that is when I realised my husband wasn't okay with this. I haven't been able to look at that picture since.

For me, the first week of Liam's life was a roller coaster of emotion. A visit from my husband would reduce me to tears and then a friend would come to visit and I would be optimistic and happy. I felt like I was keeping up appearances with a genuine sense of happiness, but an overwhelming fear of the unknown and the imagined. On the second day a nurse asked if I wanted some information on DS. They brought me in some black and white photo copied pages with horrible, dated pictures and the worst case scenarios. As I started to read it I burst into tears. I hadn't realised there could be so many potential medical problems! I thought it was just DS. There were so many people coming and going – doctors, nurses and social workers. It suddenly dawned on me why they were taking him away all the time – for testing. I felt so bad that I hadn't gone with him when they checked his heart. I felt like the worst possible mother he could have and that was compounded by the fact that I couldn't get Liam to breastfeed due to his low tone. I felt like such a failure and blamed myself for everything that was 'wrong'. I kept the paper work tucked away under his cot so no one else could see it when they came to visit, I wasn't ashamed of him, but I didn't want that paperwork to define him. I cried every day that the hospital photographer would come and ask if I wanted to buy a photo package. I don't know why I cried. I thought he was beautiful, but I didn't want them to capture the DS, almost like I thought he might grow out of the look later on. They would skulk away from my room and I'm sure they thought I was crazy. They stopped coming after the third time. I was offered a visit from someone from the local DS Society, to which I agreed, but the social worker wasn't able to reach them and left their number with me to call – which I wouldn't do for another 11 weeks. I wasn't ready to enter 'that' world yet.

On the fourth day I received my Foundation 21 (a local DS charity organisation) pack. It was modern and colourful and the kids looked healthy and happy and I read, 'Welcome to Holland' and I cried, but I smiled too. That pack gave me so much hope. It's funny, but I was so proud and excited to share Liam with others, but so scared of saying the words 'disability' or thinking about the future. I thought I was going to have to give up things in my life that I took for granted before. I was studying at the time and my immediate thought was that I was going to have to quit that, and my job. The social security paperwork for disability payment application was so hard to complete. I worried what it would all mean for my other children – the burden later on, would they be embarrassed? I cried again when I read that all males with DS are considered sterile. I worried about when the time came for school, where would he go?

On the fifth day, Liam was cleared of all congenital conditions linked to DS. While I had already announced his birth to the world via Facebook, I had only told those close to me about the DS. I finally had my way to acknowledge Liam's something extra, when I sent a message saying , 'So happy to announce that after lots of testing, Liam only has DS, thank God!' and I meant it. I knew there could be a lot more things worse than DS.

When I finally left the hospital after six days, some normality to began to return and, in our home environment, my husband started interacting with Liam until one day he asked to hold him. I took a photo of that and I look at that one all the time.

While I can't speak for my husband, I know during the first year that he struggled at times with Liam's diagnosis, but the love that he has for him is always evident. They are the best of mates and already seem to enjoy the same interests. It has been three years now since his birth and Liam has, without question, transformed our lives in a way that we could never have imagined.

There is a richness now that wasn't there before and it is hard to describe the love and learning we have experienced without resorting to clichés.

Liam has struggled with some respiratory issues related to his low tone, but I was so happy when at 6 weeks of age he breast fed for the first time. I only just managed to wean him at 3 years old! We have certainly had a number of hospital visits, a few surgeries and medical appointments along with all the usual therapies. I couldn't have imagined how I would manage that before, but somehow you do. It becomes part of your life and I don't hate it. We have been welcomed into an amazing little community of families with a similar journey and have been shown inspiration and the beauty and meaning of life on more occasions than I can remember. Our little guy seems to bring with him all that is good in the world. He attracts people and animals and we now enjoy the smallest of milestones that we missed in our 'typical' children.

So, after Liam was born, I returned to work part time, I continued to study full time and I didn't have to give up a thing. Our direction changed slightly, but it was probably always going to, and I couldn't be happier with where we are at the moment. I still sometimes worry about the future, but I realise now that it will never be worse than what I imagine, so I might as well just face each day as it comes. My main fears are for how Liam will be treated by others in the future and to counteract this I have made it my mission for as many people as possible to know him now. Thanks to his older siblings, Liam has been exposed to hundreds of people through school, sports and different clubs. He has always been loved and accepted and for that I am truly grateful. The downside however, is it now takes twice as long for me to do things like the food shopping.... now that we have to stop and smile and chat to people all the time

~Sue, Liam's mum; 42; South Australia

{Preston}

My husband and I were very excited to start a family in April 2011. We got pregnant within one month and were ecstatic! The pregnancy was so easy. I considered myself lucky since I had no sickness and felt great. Even with feeling so good, I still always had a feeling something was off.

My husband and I declined genetic testing because we both agreed we would never terminate. We also thought we had no genetic issues to even worry about (I was 27 and he was 28). We had our 20 week ultrasound and the doctor said she saw a few things but she was not concerned. She said there were some spots on the brain and a bright spot on the heart. She said this is somewhat common and we did not have to worry. She said we needed to have a

level II ultrasound because there was a less than 1% chance it could indicate Down syndrome. Again, she emphasized not to worry and that this ultrasound was just protocol.

After the level II ultrasound was over, my husband and I were nervous as we waited for the doctor. I asked my husband, "What if it really is something?" My husband reassured me there would be nothing wrong. The doctor came in and said the spots on the brain were gone. She went on to say the spot on the heart was "just a freckle." All of the measurements were normal, and given my age, she did not suspect Down syndrome. My husband and I were relieved. Even with that news, I still felt in my heart that something wasn't right.

As great as I felt, things started to change at 35 weeks. It was the week after Christmas and I was dreading stepping on the scale at my regular appointment. I went nuts on all the holiday food, a pregnant girl's dream! I stepped on the scale and saw I lost a few pounds. The nurse and I both thought that was strange, especially with how much I ate the last week. I went to get measured, and I measured small. The doctor was not too concerned but said she would keep an eye on it.

At my 36 week regular appointment I was measuring even smaller. My doctor said it was time to do an ultrasound because I was continuing to get smaller. She also was concerned the baby's heart rate was lower than normal. I was hooked up to a monitor and the heart rate kept changing from normal down to the low 100s. It was very scary, and that's when I really knew something was not right. The ultrasound showed the baby was measuring small. His femur was especially small. My doctor diagnosed me with intrauterine growth retardation. The baby just wasn't growing, and there was no explanation. I was put on bed rest to try and keep the baby in until as close to 38 weeks as possible.

At my 37 week appointment I was still measuring small and the doctor told me that I might need to be induced by the end of the week. At my 38 week appointment, my doctor told me to go to the hospital to be induced. I remember having a complete nervous breakdown on the way to the hospital. I was nervous about having a baby for the first time, but I kept thinking something would be different.

Labor was not too difficult. When it came time to push, my son came out in about 5 pushes (I was lucky). After he came out, I just wanted to see him. The nurses took him to measure and weigh him. Then they gave him to me all swaddled up. As soon as I saw him, I knew he had Down syndrome. The facial features were not evident at the time, but I knew. No one said a word about it, but I knew 100%. My parents came in the room and I asked them, "Does he have Down syndrome? He looks like he does." They reassured me he did not. Even today they still say they did not think he had it. I asked my husband and he said no. After getting the diagnosis he admitted he did think our son had Down syndrome as soon as I said it, but he didn't want me to know that at the time. I tried to keep Down syndrome out of my mind during the hospital stay. I never talked about it, but I kept thinking about it and knew it would become a reality.

After my son was born, the nurses and doctors at the hospital said my son looked great. The next day the pediatric doctor came in and said he was a little concerned with his muscle tone. I had no idea that was connected to Down syndrome. Before we were discharged, another pediatric doctor came in and said the doctors wanted to "check for chromosomes." I knew exactly what that meant, but not one doctor or nurse every said the "D word." I cried and said I didn't want anything wrong. The doctor assured me she thought nothing was wrong and the other doctors that suspected just wanted to know for sure. Everyone was reassuring me there was absolutely nothing to worry about.

The seven days before we got the blood test results were the most emotional and intense days of my life. I was already grieving because I knew. Everyone else was convinced he didn't have Down syndrome. My parents, who are both in the medical field, told me over and over again they did not think he had Down syndrome. I continued to grieve despite everyone's reassurances.We got the call from the pediatrician that the results were in. We went to the office and she told us the blood test showed our son had Down syndrome. That is when our journey in the Down syndrome world began.

I knew the moment I had my son that he had Down syndrome. No matter how many times my husband and parents told me he didn't, I always knew. When the blood test results were in, the pediatrician came in the room and told us she was sorry. She did not have good news. She said Preston had Down syndrome. I remember feeling blank. I knew all along, but the true words were so difficult to hear, so very difficult. My husband and I kept it together until we got in the car. That is where we both lost it. We cried hysterically. I remember repeating over and over that I didn't want anything to be wrong with my son. My husband cried and said he just couldn't believe it. Why us? I told my husband we have to call our family right now and tell them. I called my parents and they left work and came straight over. My husband called his family and cried as he told them. It was the absolute worst day of our lives. We both had no idea what to expect. We just knew he had Down syndrome and that couldn't be good. I am a special education teacher and I have worked with high school students with Down syndrome. I knew how amazing the kids I taught with Down syndrome were. I don't like to stereotype but in my teaching career I always said I loved teaching students with Down syndrome the most. Out of any disability, those kids were the best to work with. I just couldn't get over that MY son had Down syndrome and I did not think about him being fun or how he could be just as wonderful as the kids I taught. This was different. I was not supposed to have a child with a disability. This was not supposed to happen to *me*.

After we got home from the pediatrician and my parents came over, I cried and cried. I texted my girlfriends that I needed to talk. They could tell something was wrong. They all came over and I told them. They cried with me. They told me it would be okay and I was strong and would be the best mom ever.

That night after getting the official diagnosis, I thought horrible things about my son. I didn't tell anyone. I told my husband that I wanted to try for another baby right away because I wanted to make up for my son. It was awful. The more I thought horrible things, the worse I felt as a mother. I cried so much. I felt like I was dying inside. I was physically hurting everywhere on my body.

The entire first year of my son's life was extremely difficult. Everywhere I went that I had been while I was pregnant the year before, I always thought about how innocent I was at that time the last year. I thought about how I had no idea the baby growing inside of me had Down syndrome. I wanted to go back to that world. I wanted to be innocent again. I wanted it all to go away. To try and deal with all the negativity I was feeling, I read as much as I could to educate myself. Even as a special education teacher, I felt totally lost since this was *my* child with a disability. Reading books and being involved in therapies really helped me feel in control while I was in a world where I had no control. My son and I did not bond as well as I wish we would have. I was not in a good place for that entire year. My amazing husband bonded with my son like crazy. My son looked at my husband with stars in his eyes since the moment he was born.

Finally, after my son turned one, I didn't feel sad anymore. I didn't worry about what other people thought, and if strangers knew he had Down syndrome when they said he was cute. I felt proud of my son. I felt proud to show all my friends how having a child with Down syndrome isn't what it would seem. We are a normal family. Yes, my son is very physically delayed and not doing things typical kids are yet, but it doesn't really matter. I know hands down he is way cuter than all my friend's typical kids (a little biased but it is true). I post pictures on Facebook as much as possible to show everyone how my son is so much fun and how we live a totally normal life. I now love how I can show off our amazing life with our amazing son!

I decided to write about my son's health issues separately. The reason I did this is because he did not have any major health concerns. He did not spend any time in the NICU and came home with us from the hospital. After he was born, the doctors and nurses were not concerned about anything with his health. There have been health issues we dealt with a few weeks after my son's birth.

My husband refers to our son's health issues as, "maintenance on a car." There has not been anything major, but there have been a lot of little things. Even though there has been nothing major (hospitalizations, heart surgeries, things like that) his health issues have taken a toll and left us exhausted many times. We live about 30 minutes from St. Louis, MO where there are two amazing children's hospitals. We have driven to and from the hospital we chose a lot and spent many hours there with all the appointments. We decided to go to St. Louis Children's Hospital because they have a Down Syndrome Clinic. The other hospital does not have this. I would advise any parent of a child with Down syndrome to choose the hospital that has the clinic if there is one close to where you live. The clinic is absolutely amazing and the doctors understand Down syndrome better than anyone. The clinic has the geneticist. We saw that doctor one time and have then seen the genetics nurse practitioner. The way she explained it is they are the "quarterback" that runs all the doctor appointments our son needs at certain times. They know what to check for and when (based on health issues of the general population of people with Down syndrome).

The first two appointments after the geneticist were about my son's hearing. He did not pass his newborn hearing screenings. He had to get a sleep ABR test. This is where the audiologist had wires hooked up to my son's head and ears. My son had to fall asleep and they recorded brain waves and how he reacted to certain sounds. The first time the test wasn't so bad because my son was only a few weeks old so he fell asleep easily. The next test it seemed like it took forever for him to fall asleep. My husband had to hold my son the entire three hours it took for him to fall asleep and have the test. It felt so long sitting in the testing booth! I remember being so terrified he had a hearing impairment. It ended up he had fluid built up in his ears which was causing him to fail hearing tests. After finding this out, we decided to have surgery to put in tubes. We wanted to do everything possible to help with his hearing and speech development. He had to have two sets of tubes put in by the time he was 16 months. The first pair ended up becoming infected and fluid was again building up. Those were two quick surgeries but we combined them with other issues that needed to be taken care of.

One surgery we combined with tubes was not necessarily Down syndrome related. My son had undescended testicles. This surgery seemed rough but he bounced back quickly. The urologist suggested the surgery because the testicles needed to be descended to help decrease cancer risks in the future. My son had this surgery at 10 months.

When my son was 14 months, he had to be put under anesthesia to have a sedated ABR hearing test. This was to check his hearing. Even though it wasn't technically surgery, he was being put under which was nerve-wrecking and a long visit to the hospital.

The other surgery that was combined with new tubes was tear duct probing. We started noticing when my son was a few months old that his eyes would always get goopy and crusty when he slept. It was horrible trying to wipe his eyes every morning. We saw the eye doctor at our yearly genetics appointment (the Down Syndrome Clinic has babies with Down syndrome go to the eye doctor to make sure there are no vision problems which are common). The eye doctor said our son had clogged tear ducts which is common in people with Down syndrome. He said it would require surgery. They go through the nose and open up the tear ducts. This surgery was the most painful for my son. The doctor said it would feel like he broke his nose for a few hours. The evening of the surgery, my son was really upset. After that though, he slept through the night and was acting normal the next day.

My husband and I thought our son was having seizures around 12 months. He started doing weird movements with his head and his eyes. We went to the neurologist (with video documentation which was very helpful) and he said he wasn't sure they were seizures. One of my son's therapists mentioned it could be a self-stimming behavior. He was doing it because it felt good or different and he liked doing it. Just to be sure, we wanted to see the doctor. Since the neurologist did not know for sure, he said we needed an EEG. My son had an hour EEG test that showed normal results. After that appointment he continued the behavior and did it for longer periods of time. We decided a 24 hour EEG would be the best way to determine if it was truly stimming or really seizures. Thankfully, the results showed no seizure activity. We were so relieved.

Currently, we are still having to get my son tested for hearing since his sedated ABR still showed hearing loss (which we are pretty sure is because his tubes had fluid built up). He will have a behavior hearing test soon (he will not have to be sedated).

The only health concern that has been serious is hypothyroidism. My son was tested at 6 months (standard testing by the Down Syndrome Clinic/geneticist). With hypothyroidism it is very important to treat because if left untreated, it can lead to many health problems. With this being our only real consistent concern, we are lucky. My son has to take a pill every day for the rest of his life possibly. We just crush the pill up in his food and he eats it with no problem. He has to get a blood draw every three months to make sure the pill is the correct amount. Since he will gain weight and that will be changing as he grows, we need to keep getting his blood tested. It gets annoying to go the hospital to get the blood draw, but I always tell myself it doesn't take too long and it is definitely worth it.

So, it's obvious to see we have made many trips to and from Children's Hospital. After the appointments I think how it wasn't that bad but it I still dread going every time. It's hard to take off work for appointments that are fairly often. We are so lucky and thankful to not have had major health concerns.

Today, Preston is 19 months old. He is a very active little guy! He isn't quite crawling but can get anywhere by scooting, climbing, and rolling. Preston loves giving hugs and kisses. It is so cute! He absolutely adores his daddy! They are best buddies and love doing "boy stuff" together. I will  be having a baby next month and can't wait for Preston to have a sibling because he will be the best big brother. We celebrate each milestone with so much excitement. Preston works very hard with therapies to reach those milestones. We are so blessed that Preston is healthy and very happy! He is just the cutest and most lovable little guy!

~Lisa, Preston's mom; 28; Illinois, United States

{Jacinta}

It was my birthday when I first started to really wonder if I was pregnant. It had been a crazy time, moving house with two small children and a husband living interstate Monday to Friday, so I started to realise that it had been a while since my last period. My husband and I had decided the day we moved that we would definitely go for a third child. We had two girls already, out of four pregnancies. It was exciting to think that we might be pregnant again finally, particularly since I had thought I might have been pregnant earlier that year but despite having a very long cycle never managed to get a positive HCG result.

I did a home pregnancy test one weekend a couple of weeks later when my husband was home and it showed positive. I didn't get around to going to the Dr straight away and then I started bleeding. It wasn't a lot all at once, but was enough to be significant and was every day for about a week. I did another test and it showed a fainter positive. This got me thinking that I had probably started to miscarry. At this stage I thought I must be somewhere between 8-10 weeks. I went to the doctor a day or so later. He sent me off for an urgent ultrasound. There was a heartbeat, which was such a relief, though the embryo was measuring 6 weeks 2 days - I couldn't believe I still had half the first trimester to go!

At that point I kind of did a deal with the embryo. In my mind I told it that I would do everything possible to keep its environment healthy if it would agree to hang in there.

We declined any genetic screening since we're not the sort to act on it and didn't see the point in worrying. We did have a 20-week scan, which according to the radiologist was all normal. My home situation got complicated at this point and I didn't go back to the Dr to collect the result for the hospital clinic. About 30 weeks I started measuring big for my weeks. This continued and I had a scan about 36 weeks which showed a 7lb 13oz foetus (slightly larger than the birth weight of my eldest) and upper normal limits for amniotic fluid. The person doing the scan asked me if everything was normal in my earlier ultrasounds. I said 'yes', but I had an uneasy feeling...

Later that day I went to the Dr for my blocked ear and thought I'd get the 20 week results while I was there. I read it and saw that it there was dilation in the kidneys that should have been followed up in the third trimester....oops! I told them at the next visit and had another scan the following week to check both things. Both were still at upper normal limits. The person doing the scan was sure it was all fine and said they were both things that usually sorted themselves out soon after birth. I still had my uneasy feelings. I started talking to my husband about 'what if there is something wrong with the baby?'.

I took these two things and thought I'd google them together since it seemed to me that if there were two slightly odd things, it made sense that there would be one cause. After lots of searching I found one medical article which talked about these two things together being 'soft signs' (or soft markers) for Down syndrome. This stopped me dead in my tracks. This is the kind of thing that happens to other people and I couldn't imagine it. The thought scared me. I asked my husband what we'd do if the baby had Down syndrome. He said that we would give it every chance with all the tools we had at our disposal. This wasn't enough for me. The thought lingered for days. I finally realised that it would affect the rest of the pregnancy and taint the delivery if I didn't do something about it. I worked out that I needed something I could be sure of, that wouldn't change regardless of the outcome. Then I realised that she would be beautiful no matter what and I would focus on that and everything else could work itself out. This was the best decision I could have made.

At Christmas time I thought she was coming. She didn't. She didn't come and didn't come for a couple of weeks. Eventually one night, she started again. It wasn't convenient for her to come at 5am so I slowed it all down and I had to get her moving again later that day when we were ready. She was so ready all of a sudden we barely made it to the hospital. I was calling and calling and no-one was answering. Eventually I made the decision to just leave and the minute I got there I was onto the bed and started pushing!

45 minutes later she was out and on my chest and I couldn't work out which of my other two children she resembled. She was all scrunched up and slightly blue, looking upset. I snuggled her into the blankets and she settled down and got pink. It was when I thought I'd put her on the breast and reshuffled the blankets that she got upset and a little purple again. I handed her to my husband while I got organised and the nurses whisked her off and into the resuscitation crib and got her on oxygen. They took her to the special care nursery and I sent my husband along too. I had no idea what had just happened, but knew she couldn't be that bad. I still had to deliver the placenta so I wasn't going anywhere. I've never seen any other placenta than that one, but it was the size of a football - apparently that's large! I was exhausted and in a mystery.

Eventually I was allowed to the Special Care Nursery in a wheelchair. There she was already with an IV in her foot and she was on a glucose drip. It was out of my control. All my best intentions to give her the best start with my milk, as little pain as possible, no drugs, it was all coming unravelled. The Paediatrician had been called in and she looked over our new daughter and told us the situation. She had trouble breathing, enlarged liver, enlarged spleen, heart murmur, suspected heart defect, low platelets and dodgy white blood cells plus physical features that were consistent with Down syndrome. She needed a CPAP machine and an echocardiogram, neither of which they could do there so she would need to be transferred to another hospital as soon as possible that night.

I was possibly the luckiest mother ever to receive a diagnosis of Down syndrome. I had not only prepared myself to think of my daughter as beautiful above all else, which she still was and that hadn't changed, but I also had a friend whose son had been born 6 years earlier with the same condition. This friend of mine had searched the world and found some brilliant therapies to help her son develop in many ways as well as any other child. The last post I'd seen from her was a celebratory post saying that he was ok to go along to a normal everyday primary school the following year. I knew that she'd spent the previous 6 years working very, very hard. I knew also what results were possible. Because of this I had no fear for our baby daughter. My only thought on hearing those words was that we were writing off any other plans for the next few years because our daughter's therapy was going to be the priority.

I had to go and have my stitches and I asked the nurse to show me how to express manually and get my milk going. They told me how to store and label it so that it could be used at the hospital she was transferred to. Eventually, my husband and I had time to talk. We're not the crying type really, we tend to look at what can be done. So we decided on a name, Jacinta, and we decided to ring my friend, Kristen, and find out what could be done straight away to help as soon as possible.

The other question was what to tell people and when. My family was all gathered at my sister's place celebrating two other birthdays. They knew I had been in labour so we had to call them. My in-laws also knew we were in labour since they'd picked up our daughters from my sister earlier in the day, and of course you tell your parents! We decided to tell them that she was born, weight, time, and that she was in the SCN and would be transferred for help with breathing. I'm not sure about my parents in law but my family didn't buy it, though they didn't say anything on the phone. As soon as I got off the phone they started wondering amongst themselves what it could be.

We told Jacinta what was happening, that she was going to another hospital and Daddy was going to follow behind and that I'd stay in this hospital to get my milk going so she could have milk to drink. The transport people were lovely and as they put Jacinta into her travel unit a nurse said, 'look, she's waving'. Sure enough, little tiny Jacinta was looking right at us and opening and shutting her little hand. So we waved goodbye and she was off, 6 hours old and had already left home. Having older children who had been separated from me many times before definitely helped with this. I called the hospital after a few hours to check how she was, feeling like a crazy obsessed mother ringing at 1am. They didn't mind at all.

It was strange being in hospital alone. The photographer came past the next morning and asked cheerily, "no baby?". I was glad that I actually had a baby somewhere since that was a really insensitive thing to ask! I felt like I had no business being there, but used the time to get my expressing down pat. My husband and daughters came and picked me up the next morning and we went in to the other hospital. The other hospital welcomed my tiny expressions in their little syringes and made sure they were numbered to be given in order. They looked after us so well. They kept us informed of every little thing and were really pleased when I said we planned to just give expressed breast milk and no formula. Despite all the hope and positivity we felt, I still had strange feelings when I looked at Jacinta in the crib. We hadn't been able to hold her yet and she looked just like a person with Down Syndrome. It was hard to look beyond those physical characteristics and see who she really was.

Expressing in the middle of the night with no baby to wake me was hard work. It was both hard to wake up and sad to be alone at night expressing for my baby who wasn't there. It was a little easier in the hospital since my baby was in front of me, but not really awake.

At the end of that first day my husband and I realised that we had to tell our family the whole story and begin telling friends. We didn't want to spread the diagnosis far and wide in the beginning because we wanted to give her the same welcome our others had, but wanted to be up front with our family. My sister had arranged to come to the birth hospital where I was due to return that night to see me for a cuppa and I thought I'd better break the news before then, so I emailed around to my siblings telling the whole story and letting them know it was ok. I think the usual grapevine of "have you read the email???" went around and they all had within about half an hour. The responses were so lovely, lots of congratulations, thanks for the explanation, we're here if you need and when can we visit.

My husband had a different experience. He went over to his parents' house for his Mum's birthday. His mother's little sister has Down syndrome and she has been living in a group home for about ten years now since her elderly mother moved into a care facility. She is the classic picture of old school Down syndrome. From what I've been told, when he told his family the reaction was explosive. There were some choice words and some sentiments expressed that weren't carefully thought out. This was a huge shock for them. Amazingly though, the one person we all know in common and have a mutual high regard for is the mother of Kristen, my friend whose son has Down syndrome also. My husband told his parents about them and that he had arranged for them to see this lady the following day. This was the best thing he could have done.

We had visitors the next day which was both exciting and heartbreaking. It was lovely that our Jacinta got to have visitors like any other newborn - and this was the first of our children to be visited in hospital. At the same time, having our family there made it real and having them see her stuck in the crib barely awake with tubes everywhere was not what we had had in mind. There were tears for me that day and for several days afterwards as I felt sorry for myself and her, being robbed of our newborn experience. It was wonderful though, when my parents in law came that day. They had been to see the lady and had see how fabulously well her grandson is doing. My mother in law had fire in her eyes and she said she was on board and they were going to do whatever it takes to help her reach her potential. There are some moments in life that cement people together in a bond that cannot be broken. This was one of those.

My husband and I got working on treating however we could. We had some ideas on supplements and therapies that could be started by me straight away. We read and read for those first few weeks. I was discharged from hospital and began commuting daily to the hospital in the city. We were given an elastic two weeks as the date for her discharge. It was more like four. Her platelets took quite a while to sort out. It also was noted that she did have a heart defect, a complete AVSD with a couple of other holes, plus her aortic arch was narrowed and we were told that she might need surgery imminently. We found something we could try to help that, and it was avoided thankfully. She was kept in for four weeks in total until that surgery was ruled out.

The time in intensive care then in special care was frustrating. Expressing 6-8 times a day while looking after two other children and travelling in and out, remembering to wake myself at least once a night nearly drove me up the wall and I'm sure contributed to the torrents of tears that flowed in secret while driving myself in or while looking the other way.

The hospital looked after us so well, but they couldn't magic everything better. The day we could finally try breastfeeding was such an emotional day. It was so good to be feeling like her mother, really properly. Anyone can change a nappy or do a nasogastric or bottle feed but no-one else could breastfeed her. Turned out even I couldn't that day, but she took to it well and in a couple of days was giving it a go. The first feed changed everything for me. It was like meeting her for the first time and I finally could see her beyond the face she was wearing. The mask of Down Syndrome started to melt away from that point as I got to know her through our interactions.

However, in NICU and the SCN, it's often two steps forward, one step back. When you come off the CPAP machine it's no guarantee you won't be back on it tomorrow. Feeding was a bit stop and start because it was too difficult with the CPAP hat on. Her bloods all sorted out though and eventually her oxygen too and she was moved to special care. After another week, when it was evident she wasn't keen on the bottle and wasn't feeding around the clock (despite my middle of the night visits for feeds) she was discharged back to her birth hospital. These nurses were very mothering and it was lovely to be back with the nurse who looked after her the night she was born.

It was much easier to get feeding established with her closer to home. I could pop in and out and do 4 or more feeds a day, rather than a maximum of two. I could even pop back at 10pm without too much trouble. We tried a couple of overnight stays to see if we could get her off her nasogastric tube, but she would not wake for love nor money. People would normally kill for a baby who sleeps all night, but it turns out that in a newborn that's not such a great thing!

In the end we were so over the hospital stay that we all agreed she'd be better off at home, with us doing all the nasogastric feeding.

We were discharged into the care of the Cardiologist and to a daily routine of expressing, breastfeeding and nasogastric feeding every few hours until it was time for her heart surgery.

Regardless of the effort involved, though at times the round-the-clock intensity of the routine almost drove me mad, it was worth it to finally have her home. Our family was together at last.

Jacinta is now 14 months old. She had her AVSD, AV valve and PDA repair with a surprise MAPCAS thrown in at 4 months and then hit the ground running with breastfeeding and lost the nasogastric tube within about 4 weeks. At 5 months she was assessed as normal or above for everything except mobility, so that's what we were focusing on until about 11 months. At about 9 months she started showing signs of bleeding and bruising and since I was made aware that transient leukaemia can lead to leukaemia in early childhood, I had her tested. She's now undergoing chemotherapy for leukaemia and her prognosis is very good. Jacinta is so sociable and beautiful, she gets comments wherever we go and her sisters love her to bits. Her arrival has added a new dimension to our lives and we are all better people for having her in our family. We couldn't imagine life without her!

~ Peggy, Jacinta's mum; 36; Victoria, Australia

{Amelia}

My pregnancy with Amelia was pretty uneventful, moderate to mild morning sickness, lots of carb cravings. We were excited to find out it was a girl to add to family of two mischievous wonderful boys. We had never done any extra testing during a pregnancy because at the time of Amelia's birth tests like Harmony and Maternity21 were not available and tests for

abnormalities were prone to high false positive rates. I didn't see the point of putting myself through extra worry when I knew no matter what I would choose to keep the baby I was carrying.

At 32 weeks we had a 3d ultrasound and saw our little girl up close and personal. When the tech printed off the pictures from the ultrasound the side profile seemed odd to me and made me slightly uncomfortable. My midwife came in after what seemed like a long time and asked us if the baby in the ultrasound looked like our other two children. I thought this was a rather bizarre question considering it was an ultrasound. She then mentioned that the tech had noticed that the distance on the nasal bridge was rather small rather than a "scoop" making her profile somewhat flat. She told us she almost didn't bring it up, because there were no other apparent markers, but it could be a sign of some kind of syndrome. She suggested that it was most likely just a familiar trait and that she probably looked like a great aunt or grand parent. 'It could be nothing,' she told us.

When we left I cried in the car, Caleb my husband drove home with his arm around me. He seemed confident that it was most likely nothing. For the next few weeks I looked at children as they passed me, examining their nasal bridges. My Dad, an epedemiologist did what he does best and sent me all the research on nasal bridge markers. He gave me the odds of 1:50 with my age and one marker.

(My odds with just my age were 1:832, we had not had any quad screening done to calculate other odds)

Amelia arrived at 37 weeks, after a very quick 3 hour labor. She was very purple upon arrival and when they pulled her up beside me I immediately recognized her diagnosis. With the adrenaline of the moment, and the relief of the labor being over I felt immediate acceptance. I asked the midwife about her nose and she commented that it was a little flat. The pediatrictian examined her but didn't find any other markers. We asked him about it the next morning, and he commented that her eyes were a little close together and her nose was a little flat, but again made the comment that it might just be family traits.

Amelia was the best newborn ever, she was so calm and peaceful, and seemed to smile at us with her eyes. Her bright spirit and spunky newborn nature calmed any fears that anything was "wrong" She didn't eat well, but that is not uncommon for a newborn. I erased the idea of DS out of my mind. At her follow up appointment at 9 days the pediatrician asked us if we wanted to pursue testing, and I agreed since the question had been raised. We got the test ordered when Amelia was 2 weeks old and got the results when she was 4.5 weeks.

As we waited for the results my family kept on asking me if I was anxious about them, and honestly I wasn't really. I was convinced the result would be negative. The moment we got the result will be forever burned in my memory. I was out by myself, a rare moment, and was about to stop in at a Salvation Army store. I had texted my midwife earlier with the question, "Any news on the results of the test for little girl?" and saw that she was calling me back. I answered excitedly ready to put this lingering question behind us. When my midwife said, "We got Amelia's results back and she did test positive for Down syndrome, so she does have Trisomy 21," my heart froze. I remember my voice breaking as I asked in a weak voice, "Really?" not really knowing what else to say. I was shaking. I don't remember what else she said beyond that, probably how sorry she was, and that there were lots of good early intervention programs around. I think she also said something about, "Maybe it will be very mild," which of course in my experience now I realize is like telling someone they have a mild case of pregnancy,

I got home and got out of the car, my husband asked me what was wrong and I just sobbed. I went inside and he held me as I got the words out, we were both in shock. I was hyperventalating and shaking again. I went into our room and picked up Amelia. She looked up at me with her big blue eyes and I felt my heart sigh in relief, it was still her. She hadn't changed, it was still the little girl I had just put down to a nap, still the little girl that at just 4 weeks old had completely stolen our hearts. I felt angry that something had "happened" to her, and that it was something that could never be changed, these feelings would come and go over the next several months, year as I learned to accept this unexpected turn of events.

After her diagnosis I let myself finally start doing research on Down syndrome, on the things that it actually meant, and the things that were just myths that I had believed. I realized that i had

been introduced into a new family, a wonderful community of other mothers with children that had this little bit extra to love. Moms that told me that everything was going to be okay, and that the tears would eventually stop and this love that I was already feeling would overcome the sadness. They told me stories of amazing accomplishments,

and unexpected outcomes. They told me of adults leading "normal" lives in spite of this 'disability" and how their children were constantly amazing them. I found comfort in these stories and comfort in snuggling my little bright eyed girl, whom I wouldn't trade for the whole world.

Amelia is now 15 months old, crawling all over the place and getting into mischief. Even at her busy age of 15 months she will still sit and snuggle with her momma, melting into me like she is a part of my soul that was always meant to be there. I can't imagine a moment of my life without her.

~ Rachel, Amelia's mom; 32; Kentucky, United States

{Carl}

The day my son was born, my life took a very unexpected turn. My pregnancy was normal, everything was "great," my ultrasound looked fine, his heartbeat sounded perfect, nothing out of the ordinary. We never had any genetic testing done because we always said, "It wouldn't matter." To be honest, I never thought it would happen to us. I was 31-years-old when my son was conceived. We had no family "history" of it and already had a "typical" daughter. Down syndrome was something, I didn't even think would be a possibility.

My water broke at 2:30 in the morning and we left for the hospital three hours later. The

delivery was quick and easy; soon I was holding my beautiful baby boy. He was smaller than his sister was, weighing in at 7 lbs. 3 ozs. Before I knew it, I was being wheeled off to my postpartum room and my little boy we named Carl, was wheeled off to the nursery to be examined and stabilize his body temperature.

As my husband and I waited for our little guy to return, we were beaming, we were on cloud nine. We brought another little healthy human being into the world, we had no idea....

Next thing we knew a strange doctor walked into my room and quickly introduced himself. He started by saying, "Your son is looking healthy, but...". "But what?" my husband and I said at once as my body went numb. He went on to explain that our son was showing a number of signs that he has Down syndrome. His muscle tone was low, his eyes looked slanted, there was a fat patch on the back of his neck and a large gap between his big toe, all hallmark signs. I looked at my husband, he was kneeling on the side of my bed with his face buried in his hands, my mouth was hanging wide open, I was in too much shock to even cry at that point.

Then it hit me, guilt, it was my job to carry this baby into the world healthy, happy, and perfect. I must have done something wrong. The tears started, I remember looking at the doctor barely able to say, "I did this, I must have." He assured me, Down syndrome is something that just happens and is out of anyone's control. My husband then looked at him and told him to get our son.

I remember hysterically saying over and over, "Oh God," and, "I want our son." Looking back, I was probably screaming it. My little guy was finally wheeled back to us after what seemed like forever as I sobbed hysterically in my husband's arms. He looked perfect, we thought how could this be possible? Over the next few hours we tried to wrap our brain around all this. What would this mean for our son? For us? Our future? His future? Could I really handle a child with special needs? Why us? Why him?

I slowly started telling family and close friends the news. Our family, like us, were devastated. We all clung to the hope that there was a small chance the doctors were wrong. None of

the pediatricians that examined our son could make a definite diagnosis, we would have to wait for the genetic test. I texted a handful of close friends who responded wonderfully within minutes. I begged them not to feel sorry for us in the text. I couldn't muster up the strength to call any of them, a text was all I could handle at that point.

I wanted so badly to go back into the delivery room where everything was okay. We had no idea there. We were the smiling happy couple holding our baby, posting pictures on Facebook and sending out picture texts. Having to then tell everyone there was a problem seemed overwhelming. This was the birth of our son and felt like I had been hit by a truck. I didn't want to celebrate anymore. The sight of the "it's a boy" balloon made me want to vomit.

In the meantime, we were assigned a social worker to help us cope. Not only were we dealing this news, but we were still grieving the loss of my father-in-law who passed away just three weeks before the birth from cancer. It was all too much. We were once again mourning,

mourning the loss of the little boy we thought we were going to have.

Day two and we hit rock bottom. The cardiologist was worried about a valve in his heart and wanted to transfer him to a children's hospital for monitoring. If the valve was to start narrowing more, surgery would be needed. Suddenly the Down syndrome didn't seem that big of a deal, we just wanted our little boy to be healthy. Our son was transferred to the Children's Hospital of Philadelphia (CHOP) by ambulance. I demanded to be discharged early, there was no way my son was leaving without me. The transfer team loaded our baby into the transfer crib that looked like an incubator and we were wheeled out together. My husband and I sobbed as we drove behind the ambulance, it was awful, just heart-wrenching awful.

Day three and my son needed an IV put into a vein in his head. It killed me to see my little guy all hooked up to monitors and tubes. However, that day we finally got good news, his heart was ok. We would end up staying at the hospital for another four days. My husband stayed with him every night while I went home to take care of our daughter.

A few days later, it was confirmed, our son did indeed have Down syndrome. We were pulled into a tiny room with tissues on each end table. In the days leading up to this, I had come to accept the fact that my son had Down syndrome. A few of the nurses and doctors at CHOP made a few comments to us that our son did not "look" like a child with Ds. Those comments gave my husband and I some false hope, but deep down, I knew. Still, the emotions started all over again once it was confirmed. The genetic counsellor looked at us and asked, "What did they say about his heart?" We held each other and cried, then my husband said, "Let's go see our son." We dried our eyes and walked out hand in hand. I remember walking back to our son thinking, that's it, no more tears, we're just going to love our little man so much.

~ Sara, Carl's mom; 32; Philadelphia, United States

{Reece}

It wasn't until 16 weeks when I felt the baby move for the first time that I truly felt like I was having a baby, and I started to get excited. This was the same week that my doctor's appointment included a blood test known as the quad screen. My husband and I had debated the merits of the test as we knew that no matter what the results we would continue the pregnancy. In the end we decided to test, mostly because my husband thought it would be better to know, and be prepared if we were going to have a baby that was other than typical. I got the call a week later, and the nurse said everything was great with the blood test.

Everything continued with my pregnancy in a picture perfect way. The baby was growing and moving around like a banshee. I felt good. Yes, there were leg cramps, and I couldn't go to a gas station for 8 months without getting a raging headache, but it was so much easier than I ever

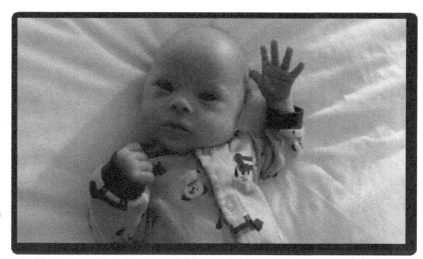

imagined. I have always been an active person and I was able to maintain that throughout my pregnancy. I played volleyball until my 33rd week (when the season ended for the year), and I played tennis until the very end. My husband and I had not been able to agree on a name for our son, so we jokingly called him starfish (given his propensity to stretch both arms in legs at the same time) or simply the hooligan. He didn't become "Reece" until he was 4 days old.

At 34 weeks, his movement slowed way down to the point where I was concerned and went to my doctor's office. They monitored Reece, and felt that his heart rate was strong and that he might be running short on room, or reacting to the cold I was trying to get over. They sent me on my way, telling me not to worry, but scheduled an ultrasound 10 days later to check on him. The next 10 days included Christmas, New Years, and the busiest time of the year for my work, but it took an eternity. Reece was moving, but it just didn't feel right. At the ultrasound the technician did some measurements, but based on the position couldn't get a good look at the whole cord, but what she could see looked good. I pushed her to keep looking- I just knew something wasn't right. After the ultrasound I met with my doctor, she said that everything looked ok, but at 36 weeks she didn't think we should take any chances. She thought there might be a kink in the cord and recommended a C-section, but as I was 3 cm dilated and soft was willing to discuss induction. In the meantime, she wanted me to check into the hospital for monitoring and to wait until 6 that evening for my stomach to be empty and her to be done with her appointments for the day.

At the hospital they put me on a monitor and discovered that what I believed to be Braxton Hicks were real contractions, and my sons' heart rate was decelerating with each contraction. So less than an hour after being in my doctor's office I was wheeled down for a C-Section. As they were prepping to do an epidural my first painful contraction hit, and his heart rate went down to 60 and stayed down. They switched to an emergency procedure, out went my husband and they knocked me out. When I woke up I was in the recovery room with a bunch of nurses, my husband and the most adorable, squishy little baby ever.

The next hour or so was a blur. I kept asking what happened, was the cord kinked, what was his APGAR, had they figured out what was wrong. Everybody kept saying he is great, it's fine etc, but I distinctly remember a nurse looking at him and saying, "I've been a nurse a long time, and his eyes don't look right." Just then the pediatrician on call came in. I found out later that she had just graduated from medical school and had only been practicing for a few months. I asked her what was going on. Is he ok? She talked about his APGAR being 6 and 9 and that his initial blood test showed that he was in distress. She was holding my son and showed me that he had low muscle tone. My thought was "duh, he hasn't moved much in the past two weeks", I didn't realize at the time that it was an indicator for T21. She quickly went on to say that the cord looked fine and they wanted permission to do some other testing including a repeat blood gas (as his first was not in the normal range) and a genetic test to rule out any issues. I felt like a genetic problem was not probable as it felt like everything went wrong suddenly, rather than being present all along.

The repeat blood test showed that he was still having issues so they took him to the NICU for IV antibiotics. Once there, they had him on oxygen monitors and found that he wasn't circulating oxygen as he should. The next 6 hours the pediatrician on call sat with us as we did chest x-rays, echocardiograms and blood tests, not to mention trying to learn how to breastfeed a tiny, exhausted newborn around a plethora of tubes and wires.

It had been the longest night of my life, and after taking 30 minutes to shower, eat and take some pain medication, my husband, Will, and I returned to the NICU room to check on Reece. We quickly realized that in our absence the night shift had turned into a day shift and our beautiful son had a new nurse. He introduced himself to us and as he handed us a copy of "Babies with Down Syndrome: A New Parents' Guide" as he said, "oh yeah, the neonatologist left this for you before he went home." He might as well have punched me in the stomach. I couldn't breathe, I couldn't talk. I distinctly remember Will asking, "Wait. What? I thought they were just ruling this out with a bunch of other things? Do they think he has Down Syndrome?" The look on the nurse's face answered the question better than any words, but the nurse quickly backtracked telling us they didn't have any of the test results back yet, but that it was a possibility.

I was in shock, but even more so in denial. Reasons that Reece could not have Down Syndrome kept running through my head. I could tell you the day that things started to feel off with my pregnancy. It was at 34 weeks and 2 days that Reece's movements slowed down, he stopped reacting to things that had always caused him to move and he stopped growing. Genetic conditions like Down Syndrome don't happen at 34 weeks 2 days, right? Besides if after treating my son for 8 hours, that neonatologist didn't say it to my face, surely he wouldn't just leave me a book. A doctor surely wouldn't be that much of a coward, right? Wait, I had a prenatal test and 4 ultrasounds and none of them found evidence of any genetic or congenital conditions so it can't be Down Syndrome. The neonatologist had spoken with us about a possible heart condition creating the issues. Heart problems are fixable, Down Syndrome is not. I want it to be the heart condition. It didn't have to be logically, it just had to mean that they were wrong.

Shortly after our conversation with the nurse, our pediatrician showed up. Reece was our first child, but Dr. Bob had been my pediatrician throughout my childhood. He looked me in the eye and said the words I needed to hear, and that the doctors and nurses the night before didn't have the courage to say. "I believe your son has Down Syndrome. " He then proceeded to go through a list of indications, like the low muscle tone, the probable heart condition, a single crease on one of his hands. These were all things that doctors or nurses had pointed out, but they had never made the connection to Down Syndrome, and I didn't know what they were hinting at until after the fact. At this point, I doubled over crying. Will was immediately behind me rubbing my back. I don't know what else Dr. Bob said that day, but I know he talked for a while.

We were in the hospital for four days. It turned out that Reece did not have a heart condition. The placenta had failed at 34 weeks and 2 days and he was just starving after a 2 week drought of nutrients. I am not a girly girl. I don't cry, or shall I say I didn't before Reece was born. I can honestly say that I have never felt so much, or as strongly as I have since Reece entered the world. Tears flowed freely for about three weeks. I have never felt such overwhelming fear; fear for the future, fear of the unknown, fear that I wasn't cracked up to be a mom let alone Reece's mom. I have never felt such irrational and disproportionate anger before. I had to abandon a shopping cart to avoid confronting a pregnant Mom with a small typical child in tow, chain smoking in the parking lot of my grocery store. Why is her child typical and mine is going to have to struggle? I don't deserve this, and Reece certainly doesn't. Sadness would hit me in waves. I would think about how easy school, friends or sports had always been for me and then I would think at how hard those will probably be for my son and I'd feel like I got kicked.

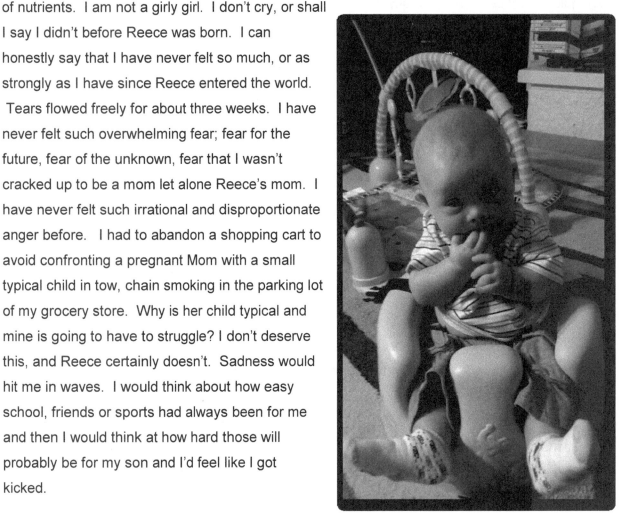

Getting the call a couple weeks later, that Reece's diagnosis of Down Syndrome was official as the genetic testing results showed the presence of an extra chromosome was anticlimactic. It felt like closure for the uncertainty, but we had already moved into the "living with it" part of life. I found community and solace with a group of women online, and now at 9 months into our journey I no longer feel like we are living with it. Yes, there are still moments that I hate his 47th chromosome, like when I had to pin him down to get blood drawn recently, but for the most part I think about it less and less, and those gaps are filling with love and wonder. I delight in his big gummy grin, and his baby giggles. He is Reece, and he is perfect.

~ Tami, Reece's mom; 32; United States

{Jacob}

Jacob was born at 2:10 am after 36 hours of agony! His birth was induced at exactly 37 weeks after an ultrasound revealed a lack of amniotic fluid. We had a very average pregnancy and birth with no complications. Jacob's nuchal fold was 3mm but put together with my age (37) there was a 1 in 1767 chance of Down syndrome. A high chance is considered to but 1 in 200. We had decided against further testing if offered it as we didn't want to terminate under any circumstances. 3mm was considered high by our local doc so we were sent for our 20 week scan in the big city. We were told it was to check "for a heart problem, as you have no chance of Down syndrome." The 20 week scan took a long time as Jacob didn't cooperate but it was all fine. They found nothing "wrong" with our baby and we relaxed again.

After he was born, they passed him to me and told me he was a boy. This shocked me greatly as I had convinced myself I was having a girl even though we had decided not to find out the sex. My second thought was I would do it all over again happily to give this little boy a brother or sister. Then I started to look at my little newborn. I remember staring in to his cute little "gnome eyes" (tiny little slits) and thinking he looked different to other newborns I had seen in photos. But I thought maybe every new one looks like this when they have just come out. As I tried to move him around to set him up for breastfeeding I remember thinking he was very floppy but to me this made sense because they had to wiggle out of their mummies so floppy was surely a good thing?

I had a lovely long cuddle with him in the delivery suite. The nurses took him for a little while to do his APGAR tests; they were 10 and 9. Which to me were like all the other tests you have while pregnant and somehow meant I had done right and my baby was healthy. I was a proud mum. I asked the nurses about his "Gnome eyes" and his floppy body. They avoided my question and told me about a cyclone storm named Yasi in Queensland (another state) that was really bad and asked if I had seen the news reports? The OB/GYN saw me the next day and questioned, "Did I have a good support network?"

Three days later still wondering about my "floppy" boy with "gnome eyes" a paediatrician came in to our room unannounced. He told us he was here to do the baby check. I thought the GP did this but mine was due to have her baby in two days, so I thought he was being helpful. He unwrapped Jacob and started to pick his limbs up and drop them, not saying a word to us. My GP randomly showed up at the same time to really do our baby check. She was preoccupied with finding the right room for her to have her baby in but asked why he wasn't filling out the forms for the check. They had a disagreement about completing the forms and my GP said she would be in to check on us.

Jacob was left unwrapped and the doctors walked out. I felt intimidated by this unfriendly doctor who was poking my child and treating him like a rag doll. He came back and said we needed to sign a form for testing.

"What testing?!" we asked.

"Genetic testing." was all he would answer.

He left the room.

I said, "What genetic testing?" to my husband.

He replied like a dictionary "Down syndrome is the most common genetic condition." I nearly slapped him!! How could he accuse my son of having that just because it was most common? This is our perfect baby boy you are talking about! How could he be so matter of fact?

Doctor Hell (the shortened version of his name) came back. I asked him three more times what the tests were for. He eventually muttered," Down syndrome" to us. I asked why he thought that. He said Jacob had low muscle tone (the floppiness) and low set ears. I agreed that he was floppy, but my mum had ears that are lower than her eyes and she doesn't have it!! He left us and just walked off with nothing else to say.

It was late that night after visiting hours, my newborn was having his first bad night that it all hit me. I had been very calm all day. I don't like the world to see me emotional. Benjamin Button of all things was on TV (what a cruel TV programmer) I realised every nurse who had popped in, to see how cute my baby was had come to see the freak show. A Downs baby on the ward for the first time in 18 years!!

That was the day my world fell apart.

I had spent the whole day hoping they had got something wrong and he was ok. How can they put a label on a three day old baby? It wasn't fair! He was perfectly healthy and just had minor temperature issues. How can his floppy legs and low set ears condemn him to being so different forever? He was my little man and he was perfect!

I had chronic fatigue syndrome since I was 15 years old. I had been in pain and always very tired for the last 13 years. Many people said I shouldn't have kids as I couldn't look after myself enough. But through all those years, I was always stronger and had more energy when I was with children. I was a childcare worker because I felt kids didn't care if I was sick, they just wanted me to play. Somehow I could always muster up energy if there was a child to play with. I didn't care what people thought. I knew I was strong enough to handle anything. You have to be strong to even drag yourself out of bed with chronic fatigue. It's like having a bad case of the flu everyday. I still had doubts and was worried about raising a "normal" kid. How could a give a baby with additional needs what he needed? Had I given this too him because I was so useless? I felt the pregnancy was the only thing I'd ever been ok at? Now I'd messed up my baby?

But I never stopped loving my little man for one moment, I was mostly worried that the world would never love him as much as I did.

It was three days before we got the 99% confirmation he had Ds with the FISH test. I still hoped somehow they had got it wrong. By the time we received the official result in 1 month, we had come to terms with it and already been through a lot with him. We didn't need confirmation. We had done the research and understood. We had come to be proud of his little differences and were even starting to show him off to total strangers. This is our baby; he has Down syndrome!

Jacob was five days old when we left hospital. On the way out, there was one more surprise. We were given a mandatory government survey to fill out before we lift because our child had "a genetic defect at birth." This form went on to ask us questions about lifestyle choices (such as alcohol and drug taking) work and home environment (such as chemical expose, age, weight). This form would be used for statistics. It might seem like a small thing, but when you have just been told two days before that your baby was "disabled," you are already looking for a way to blame yourself 100 times over. This form seemed to be a list of things we had potentially done wrong. A very long list! I have never had alcohol or drugs and tried to be very healthy for my pregnancy. I thought I had done everything to ensure my child had a good start. Now I had a list of every way I had potentially ruined his life! My husband has worked with many chemicals and was a normal young man who liked to party, so I had plenty to blame him for too. Being singled out and asked such intrusive questions at such a hard time was like rubbing salt in fresh wounds!

We got home on a Saturday. Family had come to visit so we had all three gandparents around. It was a lovely time of first baths at home and lots of snuggles. The whole time we had the possible DS hanging over our heads. I had a few tears but kept telling myself they had got it wrong. That "low tone " and "low set ears " meant nothing. He was fine. We decided not to tell anyone else until we knew for sure. I kept looking at him wondering if he looked strange? Was I the only one who thought he was adorable? How could a baby who the doctors thought was a freak of nature look so cute? Maybe I was crazy and he wasn't cute? I felt so bad for being so superficial I hated that it mattered how cute he was. But he was super cute!! I was so proud of him no matter what just worried too much what others thought.

On Monday we went to our doctor for results or the FISH test which would tell us to a 98% accuracy I believe. I told myself the results would be negative and if they were positive we still had a 2% chance he didn't have it so no need to worry yet. Our doctor was having a C section for her own baby tomorrow so she came in on her day off and told us the results. She said it was hard as she knew the results on Friday but had to wait for the appointment over the weekend. Chances are he had DS. I held it together and tried to be calm. I don't like to be emotional in public. She then introduced us to her fill in doctor. Not the time you want to meet someone new! I held it together until paying on the way out and then stood in the corner face the wall and cried my eyes out while my husband sorted the bill.

After five days at home and trying to figure out breastfeeding, Jacob had a very bad night. I tried everything but he just wouldn't feed. He wouldn't stop screaming either. I called an online breastfeeding helpline twice but the lady was grumpy and not helpful. Then I called the hospital and I was yelled at for not calling earlier and if he didn't feed to go in. He fed a little eventually. So first thing the next day the midwife brought an expressing kit and I was able to feed him. Again that night he wasn't settled and I couldn't get my usually sleepy boy to sleep . Finally at

1am I put him to bed. 10 mins later he let out a blood curdling scream. My husband decided to change him as he liked a fresh bottom. Then my husband yelled "HE'S PEEING BLOOD!!!" I ran over to see and he was right.

We took him to our local hospital. Once the nurses saw the nappy (diaper, they sent us off to drive to the bigger hospital an hour away. They said it would take too long to get him help here, if he was their son they would drive him right now. At 2am we drove for an hour. Once we got there it was a crazy they checked his last jaundice test.   It was higher than one older nurse had ever seen. They did tests and it was revealed he also had a urinary tract infection, blood infection and kidney infection. Combined with the jaundice, he was very sick. We were in hospital for 14 days and had to get lots of fluid in to flush out the jaundice. We were forced to feed him with a feeding tube. When we finally got him home, we were on strict instructions to mix feed him to fatten him up. This was very hard for me as I was obsessed with breastfeeding. I felt like a failure. I hated buying formula. I felt the world was judging me for being a bad mum.

We got the official test back when he was a month old. By then we had done our research and chatted to medical staff and we knew our boy had a little extra and we were proud of him. I didn't know how to tell our friends. It felt like a shameful secret, but I knew it shouldn't be. I started by telling total strangers as I wouldn't get emotional with them. Once I got comfortable, we started to tell friends. When I finally got to post it on Facebook, I was so proud by the positive response I got. I have never had a negative word from friends or family. They love him like we do!! They are proud of him too!

After that we had ups and downs with medical issues. The only other major one was his heart.

At 1 month old we took him for a routine check, being assured that he only had a little murmur and wasn't sick as they had seen how strong he could cry. We went in to the appointment very confident. This changed as we watched the doctor's faces as they did an ultrasound on his heart. We were told he had a VERY LARGE VSD and he would need open heart surgery.

Again our world fell apart. He had a hole so big in the wall of his heart. It was like he had the wall removed to make an open plan kitchen! They said he would die without surgery.

Three months later we watched him drink less and less. He was getting so skinny; he was a skeleton. Our baby boy was dying before our eyes.

The hospital we needed to go to was full. Three times our date was moved, until eventually we drove 5 hours and flew another hour to another state to get his operation. He needed it 6 weeks earlier. On the day of the surgery he was too tired to cry even though he had to fast all day. Handing him over was the hardest thing I've had to do. I thought they would let me hold him as he went to sleep but they wheeled him away fully clothed, awake and staring at me.

Tiny. Lying in the middle of a big cot. Six big male doctors pushed the cot away.

After hours of tears, they rang to say he would be ready to see us in an hour. We rushed to the hospital. Two hours later we were still waiting… eventually, after what seemed like days, a doctor came and told us they were still working on him. I froze and didn't get to say anything before he was gone. Later we were told that they were having trouble starting his heart. Eventually we got to see him.

The next nine days were some of the hardest and best times of our lives. We made lifelong friends with our roommates and had our hearts broken once more when we received news that one of the babies we shared those nine days with lost his life after five weeks of fighting after birth. We learned the true meaning of survivor's guilt as we came home with our son and cried for our now close friend as she went home without her son. We entered a world where babies sometimes die, but miracles happen everyday. We were there as two very special children went home for the first time after many months in hospital. One child breaking the record books for being the first to survive and go home with her condition.

We feel we handled the heart surgery well because of the support from other parents. Before we left we had four months of survival stories and hope from our local Heartkids support group. We saw before and after photos. We met crazy daredevil kids with heart scars (zipper scars) that were so healthy and full of energy it scared us. We learned it would be okay! We learned to stop and smell the roses and never to take or little man for granted. He is our hero! I wouldn't change a moment of the hard times. Except, of course, to bring back the beautiful children we have lost along the way. Each one we have learned something from and we will never forget!

Since then, apart from re-occurring urinary tract infections, Jacob has been very healthy. At 2 and a half he has just started walking and became a big brother to baby Isabella who he adores! He signs over 100 words and is starting to talk. We wouldn't change our little man for the world, but we would change the world for him! We hope this book helps change the world even just a little!

Jacob is 2.5 years. At 1 month old he had an accidental drug over dose when the doctor put the decimal point in the wrong place on his diuretics for heart failure. Because of my quick thinking and slightly paranoid mum qualities he was fine 24 hours later. He had open heart surgery to repair a VSD at four months old and was out of hospital in less than nine days. He has also had over a dozen urinary tract infections. other than that we have had a good run with his health. He is signing over 100 words and signing 2 word sentences. He loves singing, dancing and

making noise. He is obsessed with The Wiggles. He has just started walking in the last month and has also became a big brother to baby Isabella who he adores. He is a great big brother and helper. He amazes us everyday and we think he's perfect just the way he is. We wouldn't change our little man for the world, but we would change the world for him! We hope this book helps change the world even just a little!

~Rachel, Jacob's mum; 27; South Australia

{Tobin}

As I reclined on the recovery room gurney, I thought about how physically difficult this pregnancy had been. How I had reached a time in my life I never imagined possible; the point that I felt satisfied with this being my last pregnancy. And I was overjoyed at this giant 10 pound baby nestled against my bare skin. I was weary from the worry that plagued this 5th pregnancy and 5th c-section. Quietly, I chided those statistic quoting ob doctors that terrified me and only added emotional weight to the physical stress of this pregnancy. I wanted to marinate in this

new life; soak him in, learn his smell, nurse him and enjoy our couple time before going home to the busyness of life. I just held him; skin to skin while attempting to latch him on to nurse. We stayed like this for several hours, revelling in our new couplehood. And we prayed in thanksgiving to God for delivering us this sweet baby who was so incredibly cute and looked exactly like his big brother Carsten. Our elation lasted into the wee hours of the morning as we were transferred to a private room to enjoy our new son. I tried off and on all morning to nurse him. He was just so darn sleepy. By 10 am, he was taken off to the newborn nursery for his bath and check-up.

Shortly thereafter, a pediatrician came to our room. She was an exotic looking woman with long dark hair, impeccably dressed and spoke with a beautiful accent. She explained that she had been taking care of our beautiful son. She went on to say that there were a few characteristics that she thought might be consistent with Down syndrome. I'm not sure if I laughed out loud or not but my first reaction was that this woman was completely mistaken. He looked just like his brother for heaven's sake. And then just as quickly as that thought entered my mind, I knew. It was if the Holy Spirit had been quietly nudging me throughout my pregnancy; maybe even my whole life. Not that I had that full realization at that moment. But for a split second, everything clicked. I remembered back to Advent when I was involved with 40 days for life, the pro-life prayer vigil that is during advent and lent. I learned of the staggering percentage of babies aborted that are diagnosed prenatally with Down syndrome. Repeatedly throughout my last trimester; I kept thinking, "Please God, I do not think I can handle a special needs child". I do not know what lead me to have those thoughts.

Then the pretty lady who had so beautifully expressed that my son may have this completely unfamiliar condition explained that she had requested the genetics team from the children's hospital next door come to check on him. We agreed, thanked her for her kindness, (she never once said "I'm sorry but your son may have Ds), and then spent the next hour flabbergasted. Kyle thought this doctor was out of her mind. Although I kept agreeing with him; **I knew**. Once someone verbalized it, it made sense like the last piece being slide into the open place on a jigsaw puzzle. I told Kyle that I thought they were right and he still just couldn't see it. I waivered between thinking that everything would be fine and that our world was changing in a way we could not fully realize. When a small group of people entered our room about an hour later, pulling in chairs accompanied by the pretty doctor, my heart began to ache. The geneticist was very matter of fact but her words were measured and kind. I heard only a little of what she explained would lead her to believe Tobin has Down syndrome. As tears streamed down my face, she asked where my tears were coming from. And honestly I just didn't know. Mostly I felt selfish for feeling sad. Why was I sad? I still ask myself this today and still haven't quite figured it out fully. Dr. Zackai did a wonderfully thorough job of explaining the diagnostic process and asked if we had any questions. I asked her how certain she was. She said, "I wouldn't be here talking to you if I wasn't certain".

When they left, I requested my boy be brought back. I needed him close. I needed for him to feel my love. And I grieved. I wasn't sad that he wasn't the baby I had expected. I grieved over the mom I was challenged to be. I had felt like such a disappointment, in the prior months, to my kids. I was looking forward to moving forward and having more time to be whom they needed from me. And I was so afraid that I wouldn't be able to meet this challenge. This fear gripped my heart for 3 weeks. I told only a handful of friends because we wanted people to love our son; not our son "with Ds". When I told them, I asked for their prayers that God would equip me to be the mom that Tobin needed and deserved. I couldn't read any "feel good" stories about children with Ds or families that loved them. My fear caused me to be very cynical. One day, while I was absorbed with a combination of self-pity and worry about my son's future, I heard a voice stir inside of me. Not an audible voice but a feeling. Suddenly, a very clear realization came over me. God did not do this **to** us. This is our life and it happened. How we choose to move forward is what defines us. Fear is not of God. And that was the moment that was a game changer. I felt like I could breathe again. The weight of fear and doubt lifted. I stopped the daily tears. I could look at this beautiful child without thinking about Down syndrome every time. I realized, too, that this baby was mine, just like my other four. He was mine. God didn't give him to me because I am special. I am being challenged to rise to the occasion.

Months after Tobin was born, my dear friend Sabine told me this story. Nearly 4 years ago when she was 20 weeks pregnant, she chose to do the prenatal blood work test. Before receiving any results, she said she would want an amniocentesis because of her advanced age (39). She's a very concrete, intelligent and determined person. So when I challenged why she would consider such a risk to her long anticipated son, she admitted her fear in a baby with Ds.

I remember our conversation but not exactly what I said. Apparently, I told her "Sabine, if your baby has Down syndrome, I'll raise him". To this day, she calls and asks how her son Tobin is and if I am taking good care of him.

Recently, in an online community of moms with children with Ds, us moms were accused of being all "rainbows and unicorns". I think the reason it comes across like that is because the overwhelming fear that we experience in those first days now seemed so completely unnecessary. It's shouldn't be surprising that our children with 47 chromosomes are not much different than those with 46. I cannot say with 100% certainty that Tobin's extra chromosome is what is teaching me some beautiful lessons or not but I am learning lessons that I have been working on my entire motherhood career. A mentor mom I knew in TX used to say, "The laundry will wait." I would think, "It's going to multiply while it's waiting." But you don't have a choice but to let it wait when your infant takes 45 minutes to nurse because he has low muscle tone in his mouth. And when the grandmotherly type would say, "Enjoy the baby years because they go too fast," I am trying my hardest to treasure the fact that my stubborn 17 month doesn't want to walk. I think I have felt the true power of prayer throughout the past year. I am not a perfect mom. But I have become a better mom to all my children. God is equipping me to be the mom they all deserve and I owe it all to Tobin.

Today, Tobin is a healthy 17 month old whose cheesy smile can make anyone laugh. He is working hard at walking. He is cruising on the furniture, taking 2-3 steps between his siblings and practically running if he is holding someone's hand. We are working on sign language (we did with all of our children) and he consistently signs 4-6 words. We are anxiously awaiting his first spoken words. He fills our home with laughter, activity and milestones that seem monumental. We are beyond blessed that he is a part of our family.

~Troy, Tobin's mom; 39; New Jersey, United States

{Kayleb}

Coming up on Kayleb's first birthday a lot has been on my mind. I have been thinking back to the day he was born a year ago today. There is still a twinge of pain there, but it is good. When I got pregnant with Kayleb I was very overwhelmed of how in the world we were going to make it because Klohie was just 7 months old! But after the initial shock excitement set in. It was a pretty uneventful good pregnancy compared to blowing up like a balloon with Klohie. About two weeks before Kayleb was born we were in church. Just a normal Sunday. People went up to the choir to sing. Standing there watching I saw a middle aged man with Down syndrome that I saw every Sunday go up to sing like usual. This time was different for me though.

As I watched an overwhelming joy came over me. Tears filled my eyes as I watched him sing. He was getting more out of worshiping God than anyone else up there. You could tell in his eyes that he loved what he was doing. Then I thought how could someone not see him as a blessing? Something I had not really thought about before. A quick thought rushed through my head "If I had a child with Down syndrome I could do it". No more time than this thought had popped into my head, I pushed it out quick. No no no don't think that. Almost like if I

Kayleb

thought it than I was giving God permission, which I did not want to do. Fast forward 2 weeks later to a very quick labor. The pain was gone as soon as he was put on my chest. I picked him up looked into his eyes. Crying I said his name. He was beautiful. I finally got to meet him and felt intense love immediately. My boy. And then "I knew". Down syndrome rushed through my head. That day at church rushed through my head, but I shoved it out quickly. God had tried to tell me. I didn't say anything thinking if I did it would make it real and true. Everyone left the room while Kasey was holding Kayleb and I was getting cleaned up. The doctor came back into the room. I knew. It was slow motion the room was huge and dark taking him forever to get to the side of my bed and sit down. Smiling he took my hand. I knew. Most of this is blurry to me because in my head I was repeating "Don't say it. Don't say it," my mind was going crazy and my stomach lurching. He said Kayleb has some physical characteristics of Down syndrome and that they would do a blood test to make sure, that would take 7 to 10 days for results. He said it. We cried and said it doesn't matter because we love him anyway. It hurt bad. I was numb. I stuffed my feelings down.

Family came back in knowing nothing. Smiling we took pictures. It was hard to say, making it even more real, but we told wanting to get it over with. They cried. I was numb. I thought my dreams for him were shattered, my hope for him shattered. I just wanted to protect him. We went up to our room. More visitors, more gut wrenching, when all you wanted to do was celebrate your baby. More sorry eyes when you just want happiness. I didn't cry telling people, I did not want them feeling sorry for us. I didn't feel anything I was, so numb like a wall I had to put up to get through. At the end of the day I finally got to shower, with no one around it came and came. I had to let it out somewhere, but when I got out I stuffed it all back inside putting the wall back up and carried on. The next couple days were a roller coaster going from denial back to "I knew". Two doctors saying yes he does. Two doctors saying no he doesn't. We were given a long list of the health problems he is more likely to have. No parent wants to hear that there child will have a harder time with life. We had to test a lot of stuff to make sure he was okay. It was very scary waiting to see if his heart was okay. 50% of babies with Down syndrome have to have open heart surgery. We were very lucky. We came home the fourth day. And waited for the results. Inside I knew, but was in denial. The seventh day the doctor called back with his test results. It felt like we had waited forever. By the end I just wanted to know for sure either way so we could move on. Positive for Trisomy 21 (Down Syndrome) I let it out then after I told Kasey that the doctor had confirmed his diagnosis. Then we moved on and haven't looked back.

Some days are hard, but most days are great. We are just living life now. We have had a lot of doctors' appointments, this past year with more to come. Blood draws every 6 months for now to check for thyroid problems and to make sure his blood counts look good because of the increased chance of leaukemia. Checked ears, eyes, swallow study, lung doctor, sleep doctor, immune doctor. Having problems with his eyes that glasses or surgery cannot fix, where his vision could be anywhere from 20/50 to 20/200. We have physical, occupational, and speech therapy. He cannot crawl or walk yet, but works so hard! We go up to Kansas City to the Down Syndrome Clinic yearly. We are so lucky though that he is a pretty healthy little guy.

I do wish that I could make it easier for him, but more than that I wish I could change the way the world views him. I wish people were more excepting. We have met a lot of great people with kids with a little something extra also. All in all it has been a great year! I have renewed hope for my boy. He is the best baby. He is pretty laid back most of the time, but sure can let you know when you tick him off. I love his personality! He melts my heart daily. He dances like no other! I am a different person because of him. Growth hurts, but it is good. I wish I could go back to that moment and tell that terrified mom that it is all going to be better than okay and that life will turn back to a new normal and that your heart will be so full of happiness it feels like it might burst! One year ago today I was so excited to meet my baby boy, but that day will always have a little sadness to it because of how scary it was. I do not feel like I actually got to celebrate that day because of the huge shock that came along with him.

Kayleb

I am so excited to celebrate his birth today! The way it should have been a year ago. All life is precious no matter what extras may come along with it! Kayleb has taught me so much that I needed to know about myself, about God, about life! My boy came with lots of extras. Extra worries, extra love, extra chromosomes and I would not have him any other way! I have learned to find the beauty in the unexpected! Even though he was not exactly how I thought he would be he is still an amazing and perfect gift from God! Happy Birthday to the little boy I never knew I needed so badly!!!

~ Brittney, Kayleb's mom; 21; Missouri, United States

{Emilee}

I was blissfully ignorant. Not in a bad way. In a completely naïve, care-free kind of way. That's how I felt about my pregnancy. I was 43 years old and I was pregnant! I was thrilled, excited, and a little scared. Scared of all the what- if's.

I refused any and all genetic testing. Nothing. At my age I knew the statistics, and they didn't matter. At least I thought they didn't, but at the time, I didn't feel the need to know. Not one time during my pregnancy, did I suspect anything was wrong with my child. Thinking back, I realize that there were moments that could have pointed to a concern, like the high level  ultrasounds looking specifically at the baby's heart. She's a wiggler I was told. They were unable to get a good image of her heart so they kept bringing me in. I didn't suspect a thing. I was SO happy to be pregnant. The only hiccup I experienced during my pregnancy was hyperemisis. I was extremely sick to my stomach for the first 5 months of my pregnancy. I lost 40 pounds and barely could lift my head off my pillow at times. It was a horrible experience.

My water broke about 6 weeks before my due date early in the morning. As surprised as I was, my body had been trying to tell me something, just a few days prior. I was calm, but excited at the same time. As early as the baby was coming, I still didn't worry. I'm an experienced mom with two sons, 18 & 14. I had been there, and done that. This was going to be great.

One of the first things that struck me odd was the size of the medical team waiting for me at the hospital, when I arrived early that morning. I know that delivering a premature child can be risky, but again I wasn't aware of any problems that the baby would have other than maybe needing a little oxygen. I checked in at 3 centimeters and according to the Doctor, the baby was definitely coming. I started losing track of time soon after, I was having real contractions and beginning to experience hard labor pain. Time was moving too fast. They tried 8 times to get an IV line in.

Apparently I was dehydrated, and now the hospital wasn't offering me pain medication. I was starting to get very upset. I had zero intentions of having a baby without pain medication, and there were so many doctors and nurses. This is when things "got real".

In walked 3 people from NASA. At least I thought they were astronauts, or pilots, minus the helmets. My mind wrapped around itself, I felt like I was in a Stephen King novel. They had come to take my baby. She/He would need to be flown the closest hospital with a NICU. HOW DID THEY KNOW THIS ALREADY? No mention of heart issues, no mention of trouble, just an urgency to get the baby out.

It was in that moment, that I said No. I would not let them take my child without me. Everything that was protective, motherly, I refused to go any further. Labor stopped, everything stopped, so they sent the helicopter back and began magnesium sulfate to stall the contractions. An ambulance was called to get me to the next hospital before I delivered and the team from NASA hitched a ride, along with a midwife, and the 2 ambulance drivers. It was a tight fit.

Fast-forward 10 hours and a bigger hospital. Great birthing room, NICU at hand, I was happy. They even gave me drugs, and I was very happy. The first time the anesthesiologist gave me medication, it was a little too much and it made me numb from the neck down. I wasn't able to feel my arms or legs, or even move them. Instant anxiety attack, but everyone calmed me down and I fell asleep for about an hour. It's now 11 pm and I wake to real contractions. I can feel my legs now, and everything else down there. I ask for more meds, and they refused, stating I could go numb again and the baby was coming. I was NOT HAPPY. I had NO intention of having a baby with NO pain medication! But it happened, my worst nightmare. And the pain was bad. The baby was coming out transverse and it felt as though my spine would never be the same. I said some mean things, but in the end, I delivered the girl I had always wanted. She came out screaming and it was the sound I longed to hear from my premature miracle!

She looked like her daddy, blonde hair, blue eyes, strong German genes. Dave and I were in awe of her beauty. Perfect in every way. I was in love with her, and my dreams of pink frilly dresses, pony tails and giggles filled my mind. We were blessed.

I was told they were going to take our little girl to the NICU to be monitored and I didn't mind. I was so tired. Back into the world of pure bliss. The next morning when I woke, I called the NICU to see how my beautiful little girl was doing and instead of getting the nurse who was in charge of her care, I was accidentally connected to one of the neonatologists. I'm not sure how the cross connection occurred but when I came on the line, he thought that he was on the line with another neonatologist. He began talking about my daughter, medical terms I didn't understand. Something about a Palmers crease, a sandal gap and that he was getting ready to go see the parents because he suspected that she had Down syndrome. When I heard those words, I stopped breathing. I was in shock. I looked at David asleep in the lounger next to my bed. He was exhausted and sleeping so sound. I hung up the phone and sat there in complete shock. I didn't wake him. I couldn't wake him. My daughter had Down syndrome. When the doctor came in, he was so very gentle. I watched as the color drained from David's face. I couldn't breathe. I felt as though my entire world was crushing me down and I would never get back up. Every emotion imaginable ran through my mind. Every hope and dream that was my daughter, was gone. When he left, David and I embraced. We cried for what seemed like hours. We cried for every typical moment we would never have with a baby with Down syndrome. We were utterly lost.

When we went to the nursery, everything was different. Everything I had hoped and dreamed for, in a typical child, was lost. At least that's how it felt at the time. The nurses were so kind and gentle but in the back of my mind I felt as though they simply felt sorry for me. I was angry, VERY angry. Angry for being handed this deck of cards. Angry for every typical child in the nursery. Angry for every new mom walking in the door that didn't know my pain. I was more angry then I had ever been in my entire life. I was also sad and afraid, and confused and lost. So very lost. I didn't know one single solitary soul that had Trisomy 21. Not even a friend of a friend. I was now "that mom", "those people", "that family". The people you see in public, the ones you smile at but secretly feel sorry or pity for. On top of the Trisomy 21 diagnosis, we were told that she had several heart defects that were going to need open heart surgery. It was almost too much to bare. I didn't cry in the NICU, I didn't want the nurses to think less of me. I cried every time I went back to my room to rest, and I cried a lot. Probably the entire first day after she was born was spent crying. I didn't know how to feel. On one hand I had the daughter I had always dreamed of, on the other, she was nothing I had asked for. The first 24 hours after she was born, was probably one of the hardest days of my life.

It was on the second day that things began to turn around. Every time I looked at her I was amazed and in awe of her beauty. She was NOTHING I imaged Down syndrome to be. She didn't even look like she had Down syndrome. I went through many periods of doubt. Even after the blood test that confirmed the diagnosis, I still caught myself thinking it was all a mistake. Acceptance did not happen right away. It came gradually.

I left the hospital two short days after she was born. We named her Emilee Ember. I hated the fact that she had to stay when I was leaving but she was very sick. She was on high flow oxygen, a heart monitor & feeding tube. So many machines, there was almost always an alarm sounding. It can be a difficult place to become accustom to.

The NICU was very difficult for me, for many reasons. The hospital was an hour away from where lived but I came EVERY single day to be with her. I left in the morning after my boys went to school and came home in the evening to have dinner with them. It was very hard on them as well. My oldest was a senior in High School and my youngest was in eighth grade. They became latch key kids, taking care of each other while I was away. I worried for them almost as much as I worried for Emilee. I was under a lot of stress and in turn had difficulty producing milk. Having two teenage boys at home makes pumping extremely difficult. Then you add the stress of being on the road for several hours a day with not eating well and post-partum depression, it was a recipe for failure. I had to learn how to remove and insert a feeding tube into her nose and down her throat. I had to learn how to use home oxygen and a heart monitor. By the time we brought her home 40 days later, I felt as though I had been through a year of med school. The plan was to allow Emilee to come home and gain weight for about 6 months, then have open-heart surgery to repair her heart defects.

We had to see her Cardiologist the second day after coming home. We thought it was a routine follow up from the NICU so we decided that it would be okay that I went alone. It was an hour drive, but Dave had already closed his business for quite some time and was working extra hours to try to make up for it. She was given a high level echocardiogram during this visit and when we met with the doctor after the echo, I was completely unprepared for what she told me. Emilee's heart condition was worse than they thought in the NICU. She needed to have heart surgery in the next ten days. I couldn't believe what I was hearing. How could she need surgery already?

Emilee went into heart failure four days after that appointment. I was feeding her a bottle and she choked, then she began to cough. She started to turn blue so I rushed her to her doctor's office and they instructed me to drive her right to the hospital that was going to be doing the heart surgery. These were the longest weeks of my life. She was in heart failure and all I could think of was that she was going to die. I loved her so much and the Down syndrome diagnosis didn't matter to me anymore, only her well-being. This was my daughter and nothing, not a label, not a diagnosis, nothing, could make me feel anything less than pure love and adoration for her. I wanted her. I wanted her to live. I wanted to bring her home and do everything I had imagined I would do with a little girl.

Even though the sadness lasted much too long, I fell in love with Emilee immediately. Maybe

not the diagnosis, maybe not her heart condition, but she really was the daughter I always wanted. I finally stopped asking what I did wrong to deserve this diagnosis, and started asking what I did right to deserve a child like Emilee.

Emilee is now 11 months old and the light of my life. She continues to amaze me everyday. She crawls everywhere even though it's a leap frog crawl, she is still in high motion. She's been sitting up for several months now & she loves music, it's part of our everyday life. She loves to hear us whistle and sing. She loves to dance. She signs four words and is very vocal. She adores her big brothers and they love her just as much. I love her disposition and how gentle she is. She adores her daddy. They have a very special bond. I never knew such love was possible but I'm living it every day.

~ Jennifer; Emilee's mom, 43; Pennsylvania, United States

{Seth}

I am now 40 years old, and I have been pregnant 9 times, with 8 live births. We have always opted to be as natural as possible. My first two were natural hospital births, but they came with "complications" that should never have happened, so after our first two, we decided on birthing with a midwife, to ensure our "natural birth plan" was followed. We did have an ultrasound with almost every baby, and Seth's pregnancy was no exception. At 20 weeks gestation, at which

time I was 38 years old, the ultrasound technician found nothing out of the ordinary, except for the fact that we were expecting our seventh son! We named him Seth. The pregnancy continued with no complications until I was about 34 weeks, at which point my pre-labor contractions were getting pretty strong.

The midwife checked me and found that I was dilating, so she put me on modified bed rest, no lifting and lay down as much as possible, for at least three weeks so we could get to the safe zone of 37 weeks gestation. It was pretty difficult to do, since we had just come through the holidays, and my husband was traveling a lot, but our 7 children stepped up to the plate and helped with the household duties. A week later, my favorite and last living grandparent, Byron Forbes Phelps, a WWII Veteran, POW and my fraternal grandfather, passed away. My parents were both out of state attending to the family's needs in Utah and Colorado and I was distraught. I was the only one who couldn't attend the funeral. I wept.

At 37 weeks pregnant, my husband was getting ready to leave for another trip, so we wanted the midwife to give us a prognosis on how soon our little man could be coming. She said she wouldn't recommend "Dad" go anywhere! Sure enough, the next morning, on January 24th, I was having regular contractions, 5 minutes apart. As we drove the 20 minutes in to town to the birthing center, I started doubting that it was real, but by the time we got to town, the contractions were pretty hard and long. I knew it was the day. I also realized that it was exactly two weeks after my grandfather has passed away. While we waited for the midwives to prepare for us, and got settled in to our room at the birthing center, the contractions became very difficult.

By 1pm, I was very heavy into labor, and I distinctly remember looking at the clock and thinking, there is no way he will be born in 15 minutes, which was what time 2 weeks prior, my grandfather had died. I remember thinking, "The Lord giveth and the Lord taketh away, Blessed be the name of the Lord!" Yet Seth had other plans. He literally pushed himself down the birth canal by pressing his feet against my side and pushing his head down. Fifteen minutes later, he was born into the water, and promptly brought up onto my bare chest, skin to skin, heart to heart. He was born exactly, to the minute, two weeks after my grandfather had gone to be with his Heavenly Father.

I started crooning at my new little man, and stroking his wet, black hair and saying, "I love you, Seth!" We got moved onto the warm bed, with heated blankets over us and snuggled in for recovery. He weighed 7lbs 11oz, tying for my biggest baby with two of his other brothers, but he had been 3 weeks early! I remember thanking God that he hadn't waited longer and been even bigger! We gave him the middle name of Byron, after my grandfather.

As we lay half dozing in the warm blankets, I would open my eyes and look him over. I remember thinking there was something in his eyes that was a little different, but I thought surely the midwife would say something if she was thinking the same thing I was. Four hours later, as they were going through the discharge papers, and nothing had been said, she asked if I had any questions. I finally got up the nerve and said, "Does he look a little Down-ish to you?"

"Oh, no, I don't think so! He is SO strong, and I don't see the signs!" She got out one of her books and went through all of the "signs" of Trisomy 21 or Down syndrome. "If you are still concerned, you can ask your doctor about it when you take him in."

On the way home, I ask my husband, "What if he has Down syndrome?"

"What if he does?" he said. "If he does, he does."

I couldn't wrap my head around it like that. All I knew about Down syndrome was the couple of 20-something year olds at Taco Bell, and that scared me. I got home and looked things up. He had 3 of the 20 signs and the page said if they have 6 or more, the baby should get tested.

We made an appointment with our family doctor for Seth's eighth day of life to get him circumcised. In the meantime, I went go back and forth between thinking he had it, and thinking he didn't, crying out to the Lord to heal him before his appointment, if he did indeed have it. I didn't think I could handle it.

On his eighth day, we took him to our long time family doctor who had circumcised most of our boys and seen our family grow up. I finally asked him toward the end of our appointment.

"Does he look to you like he has Down syndrome?"

"What? No!" He started looking at him closer. He looked at his hands, his feet, his neck, his head. "No, I really don't think so. We can do the blood test if you really want to, but I don't see any indication of it."

"SHOULD we do the blood test? Would you recommend it? It doesn't matter to us, but how important is it to KNOW?"

"Oh, VERY important! There are a lot of tests that need to be done if he does have it, heart, ears, eyes, etc."

"Ok," we said. "Let's do the blood test." I didn't really want to know... but I did, too.

Off to the lab we went. They tried sticking the poor little lad twice, and couldn't get it, so they sent us to the hospital lab where they are better trained for babies. On the way there, I started wondering, "Am I doing the right thing? The doctor and midwife don't think he has it! Maybe we should just go home and forget about this!" Craig was thinking the same thing, so we came to the decision that we would let the hospital staff try to stick him ONE TIME! If they couldn't get it that once, we would just go home. They managed to do it on the first try.

One thing I learned about the eighth day...there is a reason the baby boy gets circumcised on the eighth day, because his vitamin K levels are at their highest they ever will be in their entire lives, so the blood is really thick and clots very quickly. Minimal blood loss for the circumcision!

In other words, DON'T TRY TO DRAW BLOOD ON THEIR 8TH DAY OF LIFE!! The blood came out, but it was V.E.R.Y S.L.O.W. Drip. Drip. Drip. But they got it. His blood was on its way to the lab to be tested. It was done. I don't remember for sure, but I think we just held hands in silence on the drive home. I was SO scared.

We had to wait for two weeks for the test results would come back. The office called me on my cell phone while I was out running errands, wanting to have us "come in and go over the blood test." I knew right then that it was positive. I remember telling the nurse, "You're scaring me."

"Oh, don't be scared. It's okay. We'll talk about it when you come in."

I called Craig and told him he had to come with me. He said, "Of course."

Craig had to fly out the next night, so we made arrangements for the kids to be taken care of overnight, and then we arrived at the doctor's office the next afternoon. We were taken into one of the rooms to wait for the doctor to come in. Finally, he did. He had a paper in his hand. Seth's DNA. He showed us what it was, and pointed out the three little lines on the 21st chromosome and said, very solemnly, "So, now you have a special needs child." I think he was shocked that it was positive.

My husband just looked at him and said, "We ALL have special needs!"

The doctor lined out what tests we needed to have and went off to get them ordered. Then, I broke down. I cried and cried. The nurse came in and tried to be encouraging, but I just needed to mourn, and cry. My husband held me. They arranged for Seth to have an Echocardiogram for his heart the very next morning. I was a nervous wreck.

We drove to Anchorage, the major city in Alaska and spent the evening together. We went to Barnes and Noble, and while my husband browsed, I went to check out the special needs section. It was pathetic. A LOT of books on autism, but hardly any on any of the other issues. I selected "Babies with Down Syndrome: A New Parent's Guide" third edition and bought it. I dropped my husband off at the airport and went to a friend's house to spend the night. I confided in her and we cried together. I spent most of the night reading the book. I felt better, if only because we have an amazing church and a large family. Seth has six brothers and a sister who all adore him, and I KNOW he will always be taken care of. That seemed to be the scariest part for most parents. "What happens when we can't take care of him any longer?" *I* didn't have to worry about THAT!

I went to the city hospital pediatric cardiology unit early the next morning. The doctor quickly reassured me as he passed the wand over Seth's chest, that everything looked REALLY great! There was one slight thing that he thought he caught a glimpse of every once in a while that usually closed up a birth, but that should be closed up for sure within six months, so he scheduled us for a follow-up appointment in six months. I was ESTATIC!! I told my little boy that we were going to go treat ourselves to a coffee downstairs! I was SO relieved!

After that, he had an eye test and the doctor was super happy with his eyes too! The ears were another matter. He had several hearing tests, and though he wasn't deaf, he couldn't hear quite as much as she would have liked, so we keep following that, but at his last appointment, he did wonderfully.

Seth's sister had some pretty major kidney issues, so we had Seth's checked and he didn't have any problems there either! He HAS been in the ER twice for croup, and we've battled it out a few times at home too. Some days I feel like we hit the jackpot with Seth's health. Some days I feel guilty that he IS so healthy, but I know he has and will have his own struggles too.

But, he is my delightful, funny, inquisitive little boy, with a little temper, and a gift from God to our family and our church. My husband says we know God put him in the right family because only *I* knew he had Down syndrome.

Seth is now 19mo and a feisty young lad who likes to make his opinion known, but *LOVES* to kiss, snuggle, read books, watch Signing Time, play with balls, drop everything, (we think he's trying to figure out gravity already), and play with his cars making the appropriate boy noises of course! He eats almost everything he can get his hands on, but prefers if I tell him what he's eating first, or he'll spit it out to look at it. He babbles all kinds of noises, some of which are discernible, such as up, please, dog, dada, mama, and some of his brother's names when he sees them, although they all sound SO much alike right now. He is right on the verge of crawling (and CAN if I hold my hand under his chest), but much prefers his method of sliding along the floor on his belly, pulling himself by his hands. He can also "walk" around the house holding my fingers. He adores his 4 year-old brother and hugs and kisses all over him, all the while patting his head and rubbing his face affectionately. He is an absolute joy to our family, and as one friend who has a 4 year old with T21 shared with me, he is our "baby" just a little longer than usual. With seven older children, I am not complaining that he still wants to snuggle up and sign "milk" as we rock and nurse to sleep at night together. God has truly blessed our family and church.

~Grace, Seth's mom; 38; Alaska, United States

{LP}

When I think back on those few weeks, they seem blurry already, but what I do remember are flashes. Flashes of feeling, thought, memory, perception. There was something like a persistent tapping that only I could hear. With each of those flashes, there was another tap. *Tap... Tap... Tap...* each time it was like a marble added to a scale, getting heavier and heavier, to show me something I didn't want to see.

It started with an unplanned third pregnancy. Maybe we had successfully spun the roulette wheel twice, but that was it. I worried about miscarriage. I uncharacteristically worried about car accidents, Listeria, everything. I never told anyone how unsettled I felt. How could I? It made no sense. The quiet *tap, tap, tap* had begun.

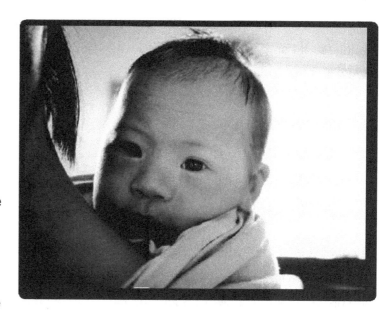

During labor, I couldn't quite place the difference, but it was there. I expected the pain, but it was as if being in labor was a one woman show, not an interplay between my body and the little life inside. When the time came to push, I felt like I was tearing myself into pieces. If I didn't keep pushing so hard, so intensely, I feared my labor would stop altogether and my baby would fade away. Later, I would learn that my baby's lower muscle tone most likely contributed to my feeling the need to push harder.

After he was born, the midwives and I peered into his little face pondering his resemblance to the family. I felt a strange pang of discomfort. Now I think that was the first time I saw a flicker of his features. There was something in his eyes and forehead that made me uncomfortable, and I spent hours staring at it. *Tap... Tap... Tap...*

He didn't gain as quickly as his sisters had. He was incredibly sleepy. It seemed that if I didn't wake him to feed him, he would just fade away. His jaundice lasted longer. Despite all this, he was all in the range of normal. But nothing felt right.

Then, I saw it.

I saw the faces of children I had seen at the grocery store, walking along the street, on pamphlets at the doctor's office. He had the face of a baby with Down syndrome.

That night I stared at pictures of hundreds of babies with Down syndrome. I learned that Down syndrome sometimes came with a set of physical markers. In the pitch black of night, I used the light from my phone to stare at his hands, his ears, trying to figure out if he had the markers for Down Syndrome. What the hell did "low set ears" mean? All babies have flattened nose bridges. If I smooshed his hand one way, it looked like he had the crease. Smoosh it another way, and the lines on his hand looked like mine.

But his face. I saw it.

The next morning, I said something to my husband. I watched closely. *Tap...* He made sure to immediately minimize it, but when pressed, he admitted, he saw it too.

I couldn't let it go. I started to read online forums, and blogs of parents who had children with Down syndrome. Each thing I read gave me a knot in my stomach. *Tap...* Even though he had no discernible major health issue, the picture they created in their descriptions somehow sounded exactly like my son. *Tap...*

I called our midwife. I felt the panic of someone standing in an open prairie, watching a storm on the horizon, with no place to hide.

Our midwife came. She said she was unsure. I held my baby and cried. And cried. That night, I went back and read my son's birth story. This was the first paragraph:

> *I think the significance of the fact that you were born in caul*
> *shouldn't be lost when I write about your birth. In fact, I wonder if*
> *you're destined to float in life with a different attitude and*
> *perspective than those around you. We will have to see.*

I found the tapping noise. All those marbles gathered their weight and tipped the scale; I saw what had been there the entire time. It was my baby, telling me that he had Down syndrome. Before we even went in to get a test done, I knew it was true.

With hindsight, I understand why no one saw it. He doesn't have many of the markers. No extra skin on the back of his neck. His ears aren't particularly low set. He doesn't have palmar creases on his hand. His muscle tone is actually quite good, but uneven.

I'm writing this now with those days behind me. I cried so much that my cheeks got chapped. The fear of potential pain gripped me. I could not bear a future of awkward moments, small and large slights, disappointments. Briefly, I regretted our choice to forgo prenatal testing. I thought about adoption. Then the guilt over being upset at all was overwhelming. Could he somehow sense my grief and feel unloved?

What I realized was that my grief came as a reaction to a world hostile to difference. As I scrutinized that grief, it gave way to an entirely new way of thinking. Why does our society value independence so much? Why is a person's worth measured by achievement? Why are some abilities valued over others? I had lived enough to know that independence, achievement, and ability did not equal happiness.

I can't choose all of the events in my life, but I can choose my experience of those events. I choose happiness. The choice is actually not very difficult. I have three beautiful children. An amazing husband. Wonderful family and friends. I have a kid with an extra chromosome. I know, as a mother, I must choose happiness for him now, so that he can one day choose it for himself.

~ Jisun, LP's mom; 31; California, United States
Blogging @ http://kimchilatkes.com/

{Colin}

I have always been a very optimistic, glass half full kinda gal. I had been very healthy thus far in life and have always taken it for granted. Our first child, Makenna Grace was born in January of 2009. Motherhood was all that I had ever dreamed it would be. That was until a summer day in June when we found out Makenna had a very serious cancer like disease called Histiocytosis.

After 2 years of treatment and a clean bill of health my husband, Kyle and I were finally ready to extend our family of three. 14 weeks into my easy and somewhat mundane pregnancy I got the terrible news that my baby had anacephaly and did not survive. Kyle and I were absolutely devastated. How could this happen after all we had gone through with our girl, Makenna.

After months of mourning what was to be...we were again ready to try for our baby. This time around I was considered high risk and monitored very closely with extra testing and ultrasounds all the way up to 34weeks. My baby boy was perfect. All of our tests and ultrasounds came back clear and we were confident we were awaiting the arrival of a healthy baby boy.

Then in the middle of the night unexpectedly at 38weeks my water broke and before I knew it Kyle and I were dropping Makenna off at my in-laws and we were off to the hospital to have our baby boy.

After an easy labor and just a couple pushes my baby boy was here!! I was overcome with joy and relief. My boy was here. He was beautiful and healthy and MINE. After a couple hours of family visiting and celebrating Kyle, Colin(my beautiful baby boy) and I had a quiet night together.

The next morning I sent Kyle to work thinking "I've got this we are good, I've done this before and my boy is healthy".

After Kyle left for work Colin and I snuggled together and it was one of the happiest hours of my life. Just me and my baby boy together, all was right in the world.

About an hour or so after Kyle left for work the on call pediatrician came in and in one sentence changed our lives forever.

I was all alone and he came in making small talk and with no warning at all as if we were chatting about the weather or last nights Cubs game he said, "Some of Colin's characteristics lead me to believe he probably has Down Syndrome".

Immediately my world was changed. Did he not know he scored a 9on his Apgar...twice???

How could this be? Didn't he know all that my family had already been through? The rest of what he began to say was a fog. After a couple minutes I cut him off and said, "I'm sorry I don't mean to be rude but I can't do this right now. I need to call my mom". He said he understood and left the room.

The door closed and I was left alone with my boy. I had no idea what to do. I couldn't call Kyle. He had been through too much already and was out making calls. It was as if my world had been turned completely upside down.

I ended up calling my mom who was on her way down with Makenna bringing me lunch. I broke the news to her through hysterical crying and she said she would be down jus as soon as she could drop Makenna off with another family member. I sent Kyle a text asking him to come back to the hospital as soon as he could. I assured him we were ok but couldn't bring myself to call him in fear I would lose it on the phone. My father in law had just been at the hospital and was a medical sales representative and was going to make some calls around the hospital when he had left our room so my next call was to him. He was the first one to make it back to the hospital and I was so thankful he had come back so quickly. Shortly after my mom and Kyle returned and all three of them were dumbfounded. They didn't understand and were as caught off guard as I had been.

A while later the on call pediatrician came back and explained his concern once again for Kyle. My mom and my father in law. This time there was a great deal of uncertainty in the doctors voice. With every characteristic he explained to us that he had suspicions abut he would then back pedal and comment on how unpronounced they were. One of Colin's hands had a Palmer crease but the other did not. His nose was kind of flat but not really....bla bla bla. I was so angry! Had this man just put us through hell and now was he changing his mind? Towards this end of the conversation he made the comment "well if he doesn't have Down syndrome....he will always look kinda funny". I was beyond done with this man who had a thing or two to learn about compassion, and bedside manner.

The rest of our hospital stay was filled with tears, great sadness and guilt. I was sad for my child. Sad he might not have the full life I had wanted for him. Guilt that I wasn't happy during this time that was supposed to be full of joy. It was as if a black cloud had hovered over us and kept us from rejoicing and celebrating this wonderful gift we had just received.

The next few days as we waited for Colin's blood tests to come back from Mayo Clinic to tell us for sure he had Down Syndrome were so very difficult. I felt like I had been robbed. I wasn't able to enjoy my new baby boy because I was mourning the baby I had planned on. I was grieving the loss of the baby I had dreamt and day dreamed about, the healthy "normal" baby boy.

When the test did come back assuring what I already knew in my heart of hearts...Colin indeed had Mosiac Down Syndrome. I spent the entirety of my maternity leave transitioning into our new reality. I spent late nights researching and learning all I could about this "thing" (DS) that was now part of our new life.

Colin has been very healthy thus far and we are so thankful for this. Colin has a bicuspid aortic valve which is a very common heart defect that we monitor but so far has not been an issue. We did recently find out that he will need hearing aids and since he is very verbal we were surprised by this.

Colin goes to occupational and physical therapy weekly and he is doing really well. At first I was overwhelmed by the appointments that seemed to consume the majority of our summer but then I remember that the reason for all of these appointments is to help Colin be the best that he can be! We have been so lucky meeting all the wonderful people we have in the last few months. We could not have asked for more wonderful doctors and therapists. It is comforting to feel you have a village of people working for you to help your child strive.

I know that our journey has only begun but I am confident our story will only get better from here. Although it has not been an easy first year I wouldn't change Colin for anything. He is the happiest, most loving baby and has added so much joy into our family. He is adored

by his big sister, Makenna and virtually anyone else who meets him. I am thankful to have such a great support system and know that although Colin having Down Syndrome is not the plan I had dreamed and hoped for I thank God everyday for blessing our family with my beautiful boy. I look into his beautiful brushfield spotted brown eyes and am instantly reminded he indeed was "fearfully and wonderfully made".

~ Jessica , Colin's mom; 31; Iowa, United States

{Mason}

A three hour car ride to Long Island, NY for my six months Well Woman Exam. Twice a year for me, sometimes three but today would be different. A new house, a new state, freshly engaged to be married but back to NY for the well planned, inevitable conversation with my long time Gynecologist. A baby, children or even the thought of having one, was not really in our future. My husband and I just did not have that drive or passion to be parents this day, or even our near future. Don't get me wrong, I like children, I really do. I have 3 great nephews, a few friends with cute kids here and there but was I meant to be a Mom, were my fiancé and I really ever meant to be parents? Not so much. It was never really was much of a thought to us. We use to say, " We like kids but we love them more when they go home at the end of the night". My visit to the Gynecologist went almost just as planned. I sat in the waiting room for the usual hour, patiently and dreadfully waiting for my turn. My stomach was a bit queasy and the wait time seemed to be never ending. I knew today, that this visit was going to have a meaning and it was time for me to finally "get off the fence" per say. I guess I should explain. In medical terms, I

had a 7 inch fibroid surrounded by a few more, living in the uterine-lining tissue outside and growing inside the uterus. It sounds painful I suppose, but more of an unnecessary burden. These obnoxious fibroids, one mainly, has led to many unfortunate health issues since it began to take up residence in my body. Let's just begin with two pulmonary embolisms, seconds away from multiple strokes, a few hospital stays and not to mention ridiculous nonstop pain. Today, I will only have two sentences on my mind. "Just take it" and "Get it out, I'm done!" That was definitely the only words I was anticipating on saying but nature had a different plan on this day. You see, this day was supposed to be the day to end my 3 hour drives to the Gyno. This day was the day where we get the exact dimensions and location of that annoying monster of a fibroid. This day was supposed to be the day of the "conversation" where I explain to my doctor that I was ready to have them remove anything and everything, as long as it just took my pain away.   Again, like I said, not having children, well we were OK with "it". My spouse and I would be "alright" because children were just not in our future. We were happy enough after 10 years, just finally being together, in the same state, a new home, with our dogs and engaged! But again, nature did not have that same plan for us on this day. "Jennifer", my name was finally called. "Right this way. Gown opening to the front and have a seat up there, the doctor will be in shortly". "Up there", the dreadful table but thank goodness! Finally, it's time. Wait, hold one second.. I'm bleeding! How humiliating! It definitely was way too early for that "time of the month", so why am I bleeding I thought. Just great! A 3 hour drive for nothing! The doctor finally came in and I immediately apologized. I explained to her that "my friend" came a bit early this month and we would have to reschedule the exam. Instead we went to her office and spoke about my next step and began to pick out dates and potential surgeons to do my long waited surgery. We spoke about having a portion of my uterus removed and we spoke about not having children. My next step was to just have another dreadful internal ultrasound, which I would have done today but instead I will have to wait two weeks, post menstruation. We decided that we can basically do the next few steps in my own state, PA, which was great for having to save me time commuting. Over the next few weeks, I scheduled and had my internal ultrasound. The doctor confirmed the fibroid was at its largest and most painful peak. We chose a surgeon and scheduled my time off from work for the procedure and recovery.

February 26th 2012 - A random thought.

That "time of the month" incident that occurred at the doctor's office only lasted one day. I thought maybe stress, maybe it was the endometriosis, and maybe I'm pregnant. Pregnant, ha! That would be impossible or would it?   Ten years of intimacy and never once a scare. It had been Two years since my last pulmonary embolism, not being on Birth Control pills and not one scare. Pregnant?? Yea right! I remember this day like it was yesterday and the thoughts that went through my mind. How can I be pregnant right? I just had both a pelvic and internal sonogram of my uterus and my ovaries. I just gave another urine sample.. How can anyone not have noticed? Could it have just been missed because no one was looking? Well, 5 pregnancy tests later, the results were there..Black and White, Red line, Pink line, Plus signs, Digital, Yes! I was pregnant! Confirmation followed a few days later by my local Primary Care Physician, my surgery was canceled and my journey began.

March 23th, 2012 - My first visit to an OB.

The visit was pretty much routine. Height, beginning weight, prenatal vitamins, healthy eating tips and then the boot! I say the doctor "gave me the boot" and shipped me off to the Advanced Fetal Maternal Unit because if my age. 37 years old, with a medical rap sheet that is a mile long. Heart Surgery, PE's , Gastroperisis , Anemia, Vertigo, WPW etc.... oh and like they said "too old" .

March 28th 2012 - My first Ultrasound

Today I had my first sonogram followed up by my Sequential Screening, my non-invasive prenatal test blood draw and our first routine visit to the Genetic Counselor. I think back to that time now and I can't help but to wish that I would have maybe paid more attention, asked a few more questions or maybe just took home a few of those pamphlets hanging on the wall. You see, my whole life, childhood until present, I have always been misdiagnosed. It took years for the medical professionals to finally make the correct heart diagnosis, the correct gastrointestinal diagnosis and so on. On this day, 3/28/2012, our Diagnosis was "potential" Trisomy 21. "We just have to conduct some more routine testing to confirm" said the Genetic Counselor but let's go over your odds". Odds? 1 out of 5 chances that the baby that I am carrying , the baby that I did not plan for, the baby that slipped right in to my life, right before having a surgical procedure that would make it impossible to ever carry a child, may have Trisomy 21? Trisomy what? 21? "What is this Trisomy 21 nosense all about?" That is all that went through my mind. Is that a way to make more money off of my insurance company? Another co-pay? More time off of work to test for this Trisomy21 thing? Was it because I was "too old"? Because I definitely didn't feel old. I play some sports here and there, I work out, I hang out until all hours of the night , I love happy hour after work, I still get "I.D'ed" when buying a drink, I love going to music concerts. Old? I'm not "too old". This all must be routine right?

"Exactly what is too much fluid in the neck mean? *Nuchal fold scan?* Nuchal translucency screening test results? Chromosomal abnormalities?

So what was next", I asked. 16 Days of silence. 16 days of "What if's", 16 days of an unbearable weight on my shoulder, unspoken actions of confusion, two people that have been so much in love for 10 years, who plan to marry at the end of next month, who lay in bed as strangers, as cowards.

April 16, 2102 - My husband's Birthday and the day we finally received our results from the test.

A new, noninvasive test. A simple blood draw. Two vials of blood , 99.8 percent accuracy , results in 2 weeks you say? Why not?? Of course I will take those odds!

Give me that test!

The results were in. Our test shows no evidence of Trisomy 21, 13 and 18. NEGATIVE. If you have taken this test before and you have seen your results, you would know what I mean by the larger, bolded font in the upper right corner. NEGATIVE! That is right! Our child does not have Down syndrome! I knew they were wrong! Now let's get back in to wedding mode!! We're getting married in two short weeks!!

September 13, 2012 - The events of the next 48 hours, will forever change our lives .

Twelve Ultrasounds later, over 30 combined OB and Advance Fetal Maternal visits , tons of sono pics hanging on our refrigerator, cool tough name picked out, baby room almost done and a "Surprise" baby shower scheduled for today and a 50th Birthday party out in Long Island that weekend. Well, once again, nature changed its course. Although my due date was October 6th, our little boy was ready to make his appearance sooner than expected.

39 hours later, After being induced, pushing through low amniotic fluid, fighting his way through fetal distress, 2 epidurals, an emergency C-section and on
September 15, 2012 at 1:00 a.m., we welcomed our 5 pound bright blue eyed baby boy, Mason Lucas, in to our world and our journey began.

Mason was brought to nursery for body temperature regulation and I was brought to recovery with some minor medical issues. Mason stayed in the nursery until the next morning, where his temperature was slowly regulated. He was cleaned, changed , fed and swaddled by a few nurses. His Dad got to feed him and hold him while I stayed in bed recovering for the day. Pictures were taken, visitors came and went as did our doctors. Fast forward to what my husband calls the steady loud buzzing noise that occurs in your ears, after a bomb explodes. You know, that whistle noise that doesn't get any louder or less noisy. The one that you hear while you observe other people's mouths moving but you do not know exactly what they are saying. Yes, THAT noise. "We suspect that your child has Down Syndrome", queue in the 4 ft. 11inch doctor , with tons of make-up and cheap perfume. "Your child has some soft markers. He is kind of floppy, his eyes are almond shaped, and ears are a little low. He has what we call a sandal gap and a single crease in the palm of his hand".

"OK, So he has Asian eyes? Well so does my sister, my nephew and most of my mother's side of the family". Oh so he also has a single palm crease". "Look doctor so do I! Have you seen my Dad's ears?" Oh I can show you a picture of my other sister's huge sandal gap toe too, she can send me one, if you just give me a second. "YOUR SON HAS DOWN SYNDROME, we just ordered some tests to confirm but we already know just by his markers"

Exits the pediatric doctor on duty.

Enter the Cardiologist. "Great your here!!" as I greeted him. "Is my son's heart ok?" Throughout the pregnancy I was concerned about Mason's heart. I thought he may have inherited my heart defect but no issues were ever found "Did you do an EKG yet? Does he have Wolfe Parkinson's White like me?"

"Your son's PDA valve has not closed and he has a slight murmur but nothing to be alarmed about. It is very common with BABIES THAT HAVE DOWN SYNDROME." said so nonchalantly by our Cardiologist.

"Our baby does NOT have Down Syndrome . I have all of my medical records with me. Just give me a second I will show you my non-invasive prenatal test results. You know the new test. The one that our genetic counselor said had 99.8 percent accuracy, which is only a small difference from the Amniocentesis. Hold on, I will show you!" "I will show you my last 12 sono pictures too!

Doctor -"I have been a cardiologist for many years. I have seen many babies like your little boy. YOUR SON HAS DOWN SYNDROME".

Exits the Cardiologist.

24 hours later Mason was moved to the NICU. While they continued to say he had Down Syndrome, he began presenting signs of Breathing Apnea, slow heartbeat, low platelet count, temperature issues and jaundice.

Mason remained in the NICU for a week as I stayed in ICU for a collapsing lung and the potential to clot. Every day became more of a challenge to prove the doctor's wrong. I sat in my hospital bed day and night just researching every site I can find on the internet. My sad, confused husband was torn between waiting by my bed side or Mason's incubator in the NICU. More pictures were taken but these pictures were almost of a different baby. Pictures were taken of Mason's sandal gap , of his almond eyes , his palm of his hand and whatever else I can capture just to so I can hear someone say that the Doctors were wrong. The waiting period for the positive FISH test was followed by a longer, less hopeful wait time for the Chromosome Karyotype test results.

The comments and questions were the biggest heart breaker:

"Are they sure?"

"I don't see it."

"Can you get a second opinion?"

"Will you keep him?"

"I'm sorry."

Not only did they add more doubt to my thoughts but they gave me a feeling of failure. I was so worried about Mason's health during my pregnancy from the medication that I was on. I worried about his heart. I worried that my blood thinning medication may have caused delays. I worried because he never showed his face during our Ultrasound visits. I worried that I the coffee clerk may have slipped me caffeine rather than decaf once or twice. I worried that I may have had too much dairy. I worried about Autism but I hadn't thought about Down Syndrome after my test results came back as a "Negative." A week later, both Mason and I had finally received clearance to be discharged from the hospital. I was not really sure what that meant for us at that time. We did not have the best support from the hospital. Our doctor's now seemed to be our enemies and our baby was not who we expected. Sure, he was absolutely beautiful and he was getting stronger and he did not have all of the potential health issues that the internet said he would. He did not really have the face of the "googled image" children with Down syndrome. He smiled, ate well, he had a strong hand grip and he rolled over. Maybe our child can beat this thing, I thought. The doubt remained for a very long time. I cried for weeks for so many different reasons. I thought about how disappointed my husband may have been with me. I thought about how I "caused" Mason's Down syndrome. I thought about his future, our future. The feeling of never wanting children resurfaced. Should I leave them? Will my husband leave us? The emotions were a never ending roller coaster.

As each day passed, we grew stronger. I grew stronger. I began to see Mason as a beautiful angel that fought his way in to this world through so many obstacles. I thought about how close I was to not knowing he even existed, as mentioned in the beginning of the story. I thought about how he managed to skate under 12 sonogram radars and how he managed to cheat his way through a fetal DNA test. Weeks passed and more and more I began to finally realize that

Mason was meant to be here. I was meant to be his Mother and we were all meant to be a family. He may not be the baby that we expected or the child we ever wanted but he is more than what we have ever imagined and we are filled with so much love for him. I am going to end this Birth story here, on one note... Some people say that special children like Mason are gifts from the Angels above. I do believe that Mason is a gift. I believe he did chose us and I believe he has every right to walk on earth just like any other typical child. I know that there will be some obstacles ahead as we pass the ones that have occurred but we are prepared. We are ready and

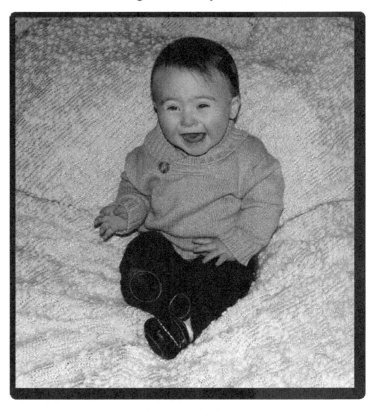

prepared to get through them as strong and as tough as Mason was when he was fighting to get in to our world. We can only hope to be as clever and strong as he was .After all the happiness he has brought us, we owe him that much. I love my little boy to the moon and back and although some days are rougher than others, I am so glad he found us.

~ Jenny, Mason's mom; 37; Pennsylvania, United States

{Ellie}

My parents always told me that our dreams signify either a fear or a desire. When I was pregnant with my second son, I had a vivid dream about a little girl. I knew she was mine, and she was beautiful. She had her hair in two pigtails and had glasses. She also had Down syndrome. My mother reassured me, "It's just fear honey, the baby is fine". At my 20 week ultrasound we found out we were having a boy, but the doctors found two markers for Down syndrome. Our little boy had a bright spot in his heart and one in his bowel. My heart sank. I knew he had it. Why would I have dreamt about this little girl with Down syndrome? An amnio confirmed Luke had typical chromosomes. Hesitantly, I confessed my dream to my husband. He couldn't believe it. He had the same dream as me. He dreamt of a little girl, his daughter. They were standing on the sidelines of a football game. She had Down syndrome.

When I became pregnant with our third and last child, my husband and I were nervous but thrilled. This was an unplanned surprise. We had already decided that two boys were the right amount of kids for us. They were 3 and 5, we were out of diapers! Our lives were getting more manageable as we both work full time. But this was happening and we embraced it. After the initial shock wore off we were beyond excited and grateful to welcome a new addition to our family.

My pregnancy was relatively uneventful except for my own personal issues, like gestational diabetes and thyroid problems. All ultrasounds of our surprise bundle were beautiful, then on my 34th birthday we found out what we were having, a baby girl. I was going to have a daughter. This was the best birthday present I could have asked for. My husband had tears in his eyes, he was convinced it was a third boy. I was so grateful and I couldn't believe it was really true. I spent the remainder of my pregnancy planning and daydreaming about this little girl.

At 12 weeks I had a quad screen done as well as a new test called maternit21. It is a new non-invasive blood test that can detect trisomies through the mother's blood. I was excited about this new test since it posed no risk to the baby. At my 16 week appointment my doctor gave me the news: baby is healthy, negative maternit21 test and quad screen is 1:450 for Down syndrome. I had better odds than someone else my age. I was so elated to hear our baby was healthy.

As she grew in my belly, her head was extended backward and touching her back. It was disturbing and no one could tell us what it meant. My doctor explained it could be nothing or could be a neurological or osteo issue. She was also in an oblique position. My friend at work immediately googled "hyper extended neck on baby" and the first thing she saw was a baby with Down syndrome. She asked me if the baby could have trisomy 21 and I immediately brushed it off, there's no way.

Then at 37 weeks I became sick with bronchitis. Our little girl was moving less and so I was sent in for non-stress tests and biophysical profiles. I had three in one week and I knew in my heart that she needed to come out. Something wasn't right. Then on January 3rd the ultrasound tech found that the chambers of her heart were different sizes. There was a pediatric cardiologist in the office that day and he took a look, confirming that her ductus has closed prematurely. They needed to get her out, and soon. We were scheduled for a c-section the following day.

January 4th, 2013 is the date of my daughter's birthday. This day will forever be burned in my memory as the most stressful, exciting, miraculous and life changing days of my life. My husband was by my side comforting me the whole way. As she was lifted from my body, I did not hear her cry. My husband barely got a glimpse of her when they whisked her away behind the heavy double doors. A few minutes later they called my husband back to see her. I was so scared. When he opened the door I heard music to my ears, a beautiful girlish cry was coming from the other room. My daughter. She was crying and is OK. I couldn't wait to hear all about her. I reminded my husband to take a picture. I couldn't wait to lay my eyes on her and to meet her. It felt like a lifetime waiting for this moment.

After he met her, he came back to my side. The look on his face said it all. He looked devastated. Through his tears he told me they suspected she had Down syndrome. I told him "there's no way, the test, I took the test, and it was negative! She doesn't have it!" I sobbed uncontrollably. I worried about my husband. I thought at that moment he was going to leave me with my three children. He was done having kids. This was my fault. He will never walk her down the aisle. What about my sons? This would change their lives too. It was all too much. My dream of having a daughter was shattered. It's amazing the amount of irrational thoughts you can have in such a short period of time. Then I said to him *"she's our girl, and we're going to love her"*. And he agreed.

That day my husband reminded me of our dream. It's like we were being prepared for this moment all along. This baby girl is meant to be ours. When I looked into her beautiful blue eyes with sparkles of white my fears melted away. When she looks at me it's like she's peering into my soul. She is more than I ever could have imagined. She is the light of our lives. Her

brothers love her more than words can describe, and everyone who meets her is mesmerized by her. We named her Ellie, which means warrior, sun ray, and light. Little did we know four years ago that our dreams were not brought on by fear. They were in fact a desire. They predicted a happy ending we never could have dreamed of.

Ellie is a smiley 8 month old. She amazes us with how much she is growing and learning. She is now able to sit up on her own and is working on crawling. She loves all kinds of foods, but her favorite is applesauce and yogurt. She can't stand pureed peas! She knows how to give hugs and kisses now too, which melts our hearts every time. She is babbling up a storm and when she's upset she says "dadada" to her daddy's delight. Health-wise she has no issues and was cleared by the cardiologist at 2 months old. I thought our life was over when we received the diagnosis, I

was 100% wrong. I am back at work full-time and am able to work from home on Fridays. Ellie loves to go boating and feel the wind on her face. She loves to giggle when her brothers tickle her. If you would have told me 8 months ago how "normal" our life would be I wouldn't have believed it. Except now our hearts are more open. We have joined a club that we didn't want to be a part of. I now see that we are the lucky ones. I'm proud to be a part of this club, I am proud she is my daughter. Our lives are better because of Ellie and I'm so grateful. I can't wait to see what Ellie can accomplish in her life. I know her future is bright. As my mother-in-law says, "having Ellie in my life is like winning the lottery" and I couldn't agree more.

Author's note: After some digging, I found that the Maternit21 test was never completed. My blood sample was never sent to the lab for testing, hence the negative result.

~ Tiffany, Ellie's mom; 34; Oregon, United States

Blogging @ www.our3lilbirds.blogspot.com

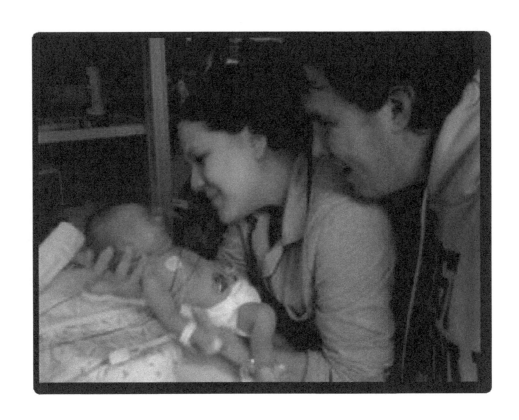

{His & Hers}

Diagnosis through the couple's perspective

Our Stories

{Samuel}

California, United States

{Cathleen, Samuel's Mom}

Looking back, I think the universe was trying to prepare me for Sam all along. Down syndrome was never something horrifying to me—more a mystery than anything else. And although I didn't understand much about Down syndrome, I had compassion for people with it. There was a guy in my junior high and high school who, in retrospect, I think probably had DS—perhaps mosaic, since he didn't show *all* the signs, and perhaps with a dose of something else thrown in, as he had some anger issues in addition to his obvious cognitive delay. He was in the special-

ed class, but we would cross paths on campus, and he was often lurking near where I was. He had a crush on me, I think, and I'm pretty sure it's because I was one of the few people who wasn't nasty to him. He scared me a little, because of his temper, so I can't say I befriended him, but I also wasn't mean to him. If he spoke to me, I

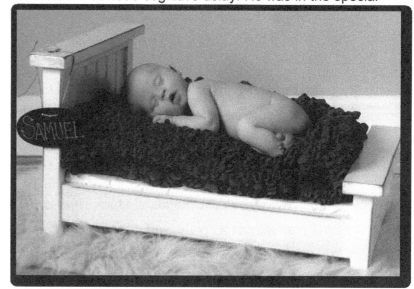

replied to him. And I guess that was enough, because he spent the better part of six years hanging out in my general vicinity whenever our paths crossed.

Years later, I was talking to a friend about children with Down syndrome, as my friend was interested in Reece's Rainbow. And we talked about how, as odd as it sounds, we sort of felt like the universe (or God, if that's your belief system) should give *us* babies with Down syndrome instead of giving them to people who didn't want them, because we knew we would love any baby with all our hearts—disability didn't matter to us.

That's not to say I *wanted* to have a special-needs child—like anyone, I hoped for a "healthy" baby. It's just that I knew if I had a child with special needs, I was capable of loving that child as fiercely as I would love any child, and I was up to the specific challenges that go along with having a special-needs child.

My husband, Chris, and I had our first son, Theo, when I was 34. Theo turned out to be a bit of a handful—he was very colicky and eventually was diagnosed with high-functioning autism, among other things. But in many ways, he's a very typical little boy, and we love him dearly and decided to try for a second child. And when I was 37, we conceived our second baby.

It was a slightly harder pregnancy than my first—just a few more aches and pains, and it felt a little different. I loved feeling Theo move inside of me, but the first time I felt Sam move, I felt a little sick, and my first thought was, "Ugh, it's like I'm growing an alien in there!" I was aghast at the thought and immediately reminded myself that this was my *baby*, who I had wanted so desperately! I brushed aside the nagging feeling of something being slightly "off," and I soon grew to love the feeling of him moving inside of me, just as I had with Theo.

When I was seven months pregnant, I was at Target one day and picked up one of their "Target Picks" recommended books. It was *Expecting Adam*—a memoir about a woman who finds out her unborn son has Down syndrome, and she decides to continue her pregnancy despite a tremendous lack of support from her Harvard University colleagues and community. I mentioned to Chris, "I probably shouldn't read a book like this while pregnant with my own son, but what the heck—it looks good, and it's not as if our baby has Down syndrome."

And then, when I was 37 weeks pregnant, I took Theo to the library in our new town to try to get a library card. I left without a library card due to a paperwork mixup, but I wasn't sorry because I was absolutely furious. As we waited in line to get the card, the man in front of us was trying to settle an issue of overdue books. He was maybe in his thirties, and clearly he had Down syndrome. He was polite, but it was taking him a while to try to figure out the overdue books and fine. The librarian, a woman in her sixties, was unforgivably rude to him. She acted impatient as he tried to settle his fine, and she rolled her eyes at me as if to say, "Can't he just *leave* already?" She was plainly disgusted with him, and I was appalled. This man, whoever he was, was obviously *trying* to be independent and handle his own library books, and she acted as if he wasn't worth the time of day. I was furious…and still with no idea that my baby, who would be born just days later, was affected by the same chromosomal anomaly as this man.

On our way out of the library, I picked up a community-activity guide for Theo, but when we got home, I realized I had picked up a special-needs booklet. I laughed at my mistake when I showed my husband later and said, "I didn't even know they *had* a booklet for special-needs activities. Guess we don't need this!"

Two days later, I almost missed my 37-week OB appointment. Theo had, unbeknownst to me, turned on the dome light in my car the day before, and effectively killed the battery. My pregnancy had been mostly trouble-free, so I thought about just skipping the appointment. But when AAA arrived and jumpstarted my car in time for me to get to the appointment after all, I went.

Our medical group provides only two ultrasounds per pregnancy—one at around 8 weeks and one at 20 weeks. But for some reason, at this appointment that I nearly skipped, the doctor cheerfully announced that she felt like doing a quick ultrasound, just to ensure that the baby was head down. "We know he is, but let's just check!" she said. And as it turns out, he wasn't—he was breech. And what's more, my amniotic fluid was low.

After a whirlwind couple of hours where the doctors debated performing a C-section right then, they decided I had enough amniotic fluid to continue the pregnancy, and they sent me on my way with strict instructions to return in two days for a fluid check and non-stress test (NST).

So Fridamorning I was back, dutifully getting my fluid check and NST. The fluid looked okay, and the NST was fine. The ultrasound tech called in a doctor just to be certain, and he spent a very long time staring at my ultrasound and making notes and calculations. Endless minutes ticked by. He finally cleared his throat and said, "Interesting."

"What?" I asked.

"Was your first child small?" he asked.

I laughed. "Hardly! He was born at 38 weeks, and he was already 8 pounds 3 ounces!"

The doctor looked at me and said, "Interesting. This baby is measuring very small. I estimate five pounds."

But he said nothing more. And I thought nothing more about it, even when I Googled "low amniotic fluid" and saw that "chromosomal abnormality" was one cause. In fact, when Chris asked me what might cause low amniotic fluid, I laughed and said, "Chromosomal abnormality, apparently! But we don't have that, so who knows." I had declined all prenatal testing, since abortion would've never been a consideration for us anyway, but I just assumed that because my 20-week ultrasound had showed nothing amiss, our baby was developing typically.

Later that very night my water broke, so I went in for my C-section 16 days earlier than planned—at 37 weeks and 2 days gestation. The doctors on staff wanted to wait to perform my C-section until morning—both so they could get some rest and because I had eaten dinner and still had food in my stomach. But the baby had other plans. After two hours of labor (and still four hours before the planned C-section), I was hit with a *monster* contraction that wouldn't end. I was near tears with the pain, and then suddenly alarms started going off, and people swarmed into the room.

"What's happening?" I asked, terrified. Alarms everywhere. People everywhere, yelling at me to roll this way and that, turn over here and spread my legs there. An oxygen mask slapped on my face. I looked at the fetal monitor and saw that the baby's beautiful heart rate of 150-ish had plummeted to 34. Yes, 34. And it wasn't coming back up. Someone turned the monitor away from me as I began to sob, "Get him out! You need to get him out safely!"

The next thing I knew, we were racing down the hallway. "Code C in Labor and Delivery!" was being announced over the PA system. "Code C!"

"Is he okay? Will he be okay?" I kept asking. No one would answer. Finally, someone said, "That's what we need to find out. We're going to need to put you under full sedation for an emergency C-section." I wept.

But when they slid me from my gurney onto the operating table, a little miracle happened. The fetal monitor started picking up—that beautiful heartbeat was back! I wept in relief. They were able to do a standard C-section at that point, and within about 20 minutes, I heard the lusty cry of my newborn son and the doctor proclaim, "He's a bald one!" And I wept as I heard "APGAR of 9." He was safe. He was healthy.

And then the doctor attending the baby came over and bluntly announced, "I need to tell you this because you're scheduled to have your tubes tied. I'm concerned about some issues of tone with the baby."

"What? You mean jaundice?" I asked, thinking she meant *skin* tone.

"No," she replied bluntly. "Muscle tone. Your baby shows the signs of Down syndrome. So I need to know whether you still want your tubes tied."

Shock. Anger. This woman was acting as if my baby was somehow "broken," and I'd want to keep my tubes intact to try again for another "non-broken" baby. What did she mean: "Whoops, this one's no good! Want to try again for another?" My protective instinct came out in full force, and I said icily, "Yes, please go ahead and tie my tubes. This is the baby I was meant to have."

Tears leaked out of my eyes as I lay there, my insides spread open for the rest of my procedure. They brought me the baby, and my heart soared and ached all at once. He was alive, and he was beautiful and precious and mine! But this thoughtless woman had just treated him as if he were less than perfect, and I knew in my heart that she would be only the first of many people to treat him that way. I knew the world could be a cruel and unaccepting place, and I had just brought a beautiful new life into a world that would likely be hurtful to him. I loved him with all my heart...but I couldn't help but wonder, was I selfish to have ignored prenatal testing and brought him into a cruel world? Would I have been a better mother *not* to bring him into the world? I felt confused and overwhelmed—brimming with love but battered by confusion.

And how *dare* this doctor mar the moments after my son's birth that way? I realize she was doing her job, but I still ache to this day when I think about it. She didn't even take a moment to congratulate us or to tell us he was beautiful. It was all about his disability, immediately. My beautiful, sweet baby was secondary to an ugly term called "Down syndrome." Was this how everyone would see him—as a disability or condition first, and a baby second? The thought overwhelmed me. I saw him as a beautiful shining light, and I wanted everyone else to see him that way, too.

Waiting for the baby to come back from being bathed and checked out was the longest 90 minutes of my life. I lay there in the recovery room, alone and with tears leaking down my face, Googling everything I could about Down syndrome on my phone. Not my best idea—the Internet can be a scary place if you're looking for information on Down syndrome! But when Chris (who I had sent with the baby) wheeled him into the recovery room 90 minutes later, I forgot all my fears. He placed the baby in my arms, and I held my sweet little sunshine for the first time. He snuggled right down into me contentedly, and I felt peace along with my confusion. My son might have an extra chromosome, but oh, how I loved him already!

We named him then—we hadn't chosen a name before he was born. He is Samuel, which means "God listened." Because God *did* listen. I'm not a religious person, but I threw a prayer up to God when Sam's heartbeat was dangerously low, and He listened. And 18 months later, that name is even more appropriate, because God really, *really* listened. He gave us a baby who changed our lives for the better. He gave us the baby we never knew we wanted, but who we absolutely cherish and could not live without. Confusion and shock about his diagnosis are long gone, replaced with the brightest love I've ever felt.

People sometimes accuse us in the Down syndrome community of painting the condition with rainbows and unicorns—making it seem like something wonderful and special, and ignoring the concerns that go along with it. Truthfully, I don't think *any* parent of a child with Down syndrome ignores the concerns that go along with it. We're all well aware that yes, there are medical issues we may have to face—heart problems, digestive issues, higher incidence of leukemia, and so on. Believe me, we worry every time our child gets a funny rash or unusual blood-work results. And yes, we worry about people treating our child unfairly, due to his perceived differences. And yes, we wonder what effect our child's cognitive delays will have on his life long-term. But *every* parent worries—that is not unique to the special-needs community. Perhaps we just worry about different things.

And the truth is that along with the worries come joy and beauty. Sam has taught us so much already. He has taught us how to celebrate the tiny joys and triumphs—the ones that we never even stopped to consider before having a child with Down syndrome. *He took a bite of solid food—rejoice! He finally pulled to standing at 17 months—celebrate! He picked up a cup of water and purposely dumped it on the floor, then set the cup back down—what awesome fine-motor skills!* He has taught us how to slow down and simply go with the flow, rather than focusing on the next big milestone or goal. *He'll walk someday—when it happens, it happens.* He has taught us that there is no one-size-fits-all approach to life and that the best-laid plans are meant to be torn apart and scattered to the wind sometimes. He has taught us to love unabashedly and freely, without reserve—who can resist a toddler that gives any random stranger a full-body smile, complete with million-dollar grin, waving arms, and kicking feet? Sam greets everyone as if he's just met his biggest hero—it's completely awesome. And having Sam has introduced to us a whole world of fascinating, diverse, and wonderful people—both those with Down syndrome and those who love them.

If a future pregnancy were still an option for us, would I do prenatal testing this time around? Yes, I would—only to be prepared in case the baby had a serious medical condition at birth. We dodged a bullet with Sam—he was physically healthy from birth, but that isn't always the case in babies with Down syndrome. But do I wish I'd had prenatal testing when I was carrying Sam? Not for a second. I am *so* glad we chose to skip it, because if I had known I was carrying a baby with Down syndrome, I would've spent my pregnancy terrified of the unknown. In the abstract, I knew I could love and care for a child with Down syndrome, but when it comes down to real life, I would've been scared out of my mind as I waited for him to be born. Instead of enjoying my final pregnancy, I would've been a nervous wreck, because I didn't *really* know what Down syndrome was like. Now I do—and I know there's nothing to fear about Down syndrome itself. There's concern about the related medical issues, but most of those can be dealt with—even heart surgery is somewhat routine now. But when you talk about Down syndrome itself, I now know that it's not scary; rather, it can be beautiful in ways you never imagined, and your life can be so very enriched because of it.

Sam is now 18 months old and the light of all of our lives. Chris has commented on numerous occasions that Sam has made him a better father to *both* of our sons. I am happier and more content than I have ever been in my life, and Sam is a big part of that. And Theo—well, Theo has just blossomed as a big brother. My impatient, volatile, brilliant little five-year-old slows down and becomes a tender, compassionate, patient teacher for his little brother. He delights in Sam, and Sam is the first person he wants to see every morning and the first person he wants to share things with.

And Sam himself? He's a happy, silly, sweet, and, yes, temperamental little boy. He is a determined little monkey who aspires to steal anything he can find and throw it into the toilet. He loves music and will dance like crazy if Theo puts on the Spice Girls. He's fascinated by our dogs and a big devotee of *Baby Signing Time*. Oh, and he hates therapy. He will attempt to pull every clever ploy in the book to get out of physical and occupational therapy, whether that means flirting with his therapist to try to distract her with hugs, crawling away as fast as he can, or sticking out his lower lip and throwing a full-blown tantrum. He's a master at avoiding what he doesn't want to do. In other words, he's a very typical toddler!

Thank you, Samuel Ames, for opening our eyes…and continuing to open them every day.

{Chris, Samuel's Dad}

It's difficult to revisit the moment my son was diagnosed with Down syndrome. Or, at least, the moment the doctors told us they were concerned about some "tonal issues." You see, the moments before that one were joyous and full of relief, as we'd witnessed the birth of our son after a harrowing delivery. The moments when most parents start to wonder about their child's future, choose his name, or figure out whose eyes he has. Typical moments.

Birth...

My wife had always told me that if she was going to have kids, she wanted to do it before she turned 40 because the risk of DS was so much higher after that age. When we conceived our second baby, she was 37; it looked like we were in the clear. We even opted out of genetic testing because the odds of DS were low and the miscarriage risk was comparatively high. (She was showing signs of early menopause before the pregnancy, so we didn't want to risk losing what might be our last chance to have a baby.) It's not to say we went into it blindly—we discussed the possibility of DS, and we were clear that we'd love our child no matter what. Not that we *expected* anything to happen, mind you.

That night, we drove to the hospital around midnight, after my wife's water broke and contractions started. The baby was breech, so we were looking at a C-section. After about an hour of waiting in the prep room, though, Cathleen had a really long, odd contraction, and the baby's heart rate plummeted. The doctors and nurses intervened quickly, whisking her away to the operating room. No one knew what was going on, only that they were both in danger. All I could do was stand out in the hallway and pray for their safety. Soon enough, everything stabilized. A nurse took me to my wife's bedside, and a few minutes later we listened as the doctor announced we had a healthy son.

The nurses carried our son into view, and then over to various machines to weigh and measure him. He looked just like the 3D ultrasound image we'd had taken a couple months earlier—

much like his brother, in fact—and had this quivering little cry. As my wife was getting stitched up, I went over whispered to him that it was OK and held his hand. He settled down when he heard me, and I breathed a huge sigh of relief, knowing my son was safe and everything was indeed OK.

Diagnosis…

I went back to check on my wife. The doctors were preparing to do her tubal ligation, which we'd arranged well in advance because we considered our family complete now. But one of the doctors suddenly interrupted and said she had concerns about some "tonal issues," so we might want to reconsider. We weren't quite sure what she meant until she clarified that he had "markers for Down syndrome." Our life changed in that instant, and we had to start making decisions immediately. We simultaneously responded that we wanted to go ahead with the ligation, rejecting the doctor's implication that we might want to keep our options open because this baby was damaged, and telling those in the room that DS didn't matter—that our son was a welcome member of our family, perfect as he was.

But that was on the outside. On the inside? I hurt—terribly. I tried to put on a good face, but it was an empty gesture. I just hurt. And I was afraid, of what I knew about DS and what I didn't know. The bottom line was that for five minutes, our son *was* typical to us. I don't mourn what he would have been—I mourn what he actually *was*, in my mind. That child was real—I talked to him and held his hand—and he was pulled away as soon as I met him. And so much of me still hurts for that loss. But when I remember we almost lost him, it hurts a little less.

That night, we named our son Samuel because it means "God listened." He did that night. He has all along.

Now…

Sam is 17 months old now and recently appeared in his first commercial for Gymboree. Yes, a commercial. We certainly thought he was cute, but how many babies have a modeling contract and work permit before they can crawl? The other day, he pulled to standing on my wife's knees, cackling as he fell back on his bottom and babbling "ma-ma-ma-ma-ma" in my wife's direction. Sam is a true joy, and he's made me a better husband, father, and person in so many ways. And for him, that's typical.

{Gianluca}

Illinois, United States

{Jenny, Gianluca's Mom}

When I found out I was pregnant with my second baby, I was ecstatic and surprised! We had been trying for a year, and recently decided not to focus on getting pregnant since we were just so busy. But there I was, pregnant!

I was 36 years old, which they called advanced maternal age, and I joked that I was an elderly pregnant lady. We knew we wanted prenatal testing; I was a planner and wanted to know everything! I had to go to great lengths to get the quad screening approved through my insurance company, and eventually we had the results that we had a reduced risk for Down syndrome (1:538).

Three days after the testing, a series of complications began. At 13 weeks I almost lost my baby due to a 6 cm tear in my placenta and spent 6 weeks on bedrest. At 22 weeks my baby was diagnosed with an atrial septal aneurism. At 36 weeks, I failed a biophysical and was hospitalized for observation.

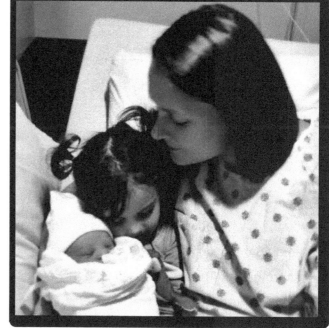

At 39 weeks, my water broke and I was so relieved. It was time to have this baby and put the stress and worry behind us. Well, as much as you can do that as a parent, but it seemed the big stuff would be behind us.

After a quick and easy labor, my son was born and I was ready to feel relief. But he wasn't crying so of course I was worried. They assured me that he was fine, his APGAR scores were great, and there was nothing to worry about. When they handed me my son I was instantly in love and so relieved that he was here. They took him away for the usual pediatrician evaluation, and we sent out messages to friends and family that our perfect son had arrived. I could finally exhale. My parents arrived with our daughter and we were so happy to see them all as we'd been looking forward to Luca meeting his sister. Our family would be complete.

Shortly after the nurse returned Luca to us, the doctor came in and abruptly asked everyone to leave the room. He sat down on the bed and told us that Luca exhibited soft markers for Trisomy 21, Down syndrome. I was in shock. He showed us the palmar crease on his hand and said it could be a sign, but could also just run in families. We immediately studied our own palms and willed our creases to merge. He showed us the sandal gap and we ripped off our socks and swore we had a big gap between our toes as well. He explained that the shape of his eyes and his lower tone were also soft markers, but he really could not make the diagnosis. He said that in some cases, he could tell the parents with confidence in this conversation that their baby had Down syndrome, but he didn't have that confidence in this case and would need the results of a blood test (FISH test) to be sure. The results in 3 days, our first day at home, so they would call us sometime that day. I immediately panicked about how we would keep family away until we heard the news because I was so emotional and unsure and scared, and just didn't want anyone to know until we were certain. I snapped out of it when he told me not to worry, that we would love our baby no matter what. Anger surged up in me at him for saying this to me. I never doubted that I would love my baby. It just seemed like such a cavalier statement to make at the time. I think he was trying to reassure us, but it stood out as rude.

Our heads were spinning. At some point in the conversation my mom forced her way into the room. Later she told me she suspected Luca had Ds from the way he felt when she held him. She's a retired nurse, so I knew she was right, even though I didn't want to believe it. She knew that when the doctor kicked them out and looked so serious that something was up. I was glad she came in because I was in such shock that I didn't know what to say or do.

My mind flashed back two years prior, when we were at a birthday party and there was a little boy there with Down syndrome. As my friend shared that his diagnosis came at birth, I remember thinking- that would be the worst. To be told at birth that your child has Down syndrome. And here I was, sitting in this hospital room, facing a Down syndrome diagnosis. I wanted to know why this was happening to us. How could this be our story? At some point, in the quiet of the night, as I held my son in my arms, I knew why this was happening to us- we were the right parents for him. We could do so much for him and others with Down syndrome. Suddenly this fight roared up within me and I knew I just wanted to be his proud mother.

When my daughter came into the room, she climbed right up into bed with Luca and me, demanded to hold him, and gave him the biggest hug. My heart melted. Holding back the tears,

I knew in that moment I had so much to learn from my kids. She showed me what true love looked like and I held them both so tight at that moment.

We weren't able to go home as planned because Luca wasn't maintaining his body temperature. As we waited to find out the results, my husband and I spent all our time with Luca. We would stare at him, pray over him, snuggle him extra long and just let our hearts connect with his. I wavered between believing he had Ds, and believing he didn't; exploring both sets of emotions. We bonded with him in such a special way those early days which was very important.

While we were sitting by him in the SCN one night, an overnight nurse started up a conversation with us. When we shared that the FISH results were not yet in, she blurted that her friend was a genetic counselor and it was unbelievable the things they find in those tests; all sorts of chromosomal anomalies that you wouldn't believe; stuff that kills babies. Our hearts sank and we were scared. She was behind a computer and couldn't see the terrified looks on our faces. It was in that moment I realized I didn't care if he had Down syndrome. I just didn't want to lose him!

It was a Friday morning, I had just gotten out of the shower and was blow drying my hair when our pediatrician came in. She had a serious look on her face so I stopped with half a head of wet hair, and sat down on the couch next to my husband. She then told us she had the results of the blood test, and Luca tested positive for Trisomy 21, Down syndrome. That was it. She asked if we had any questions. Just as she finished talking, my mom called and I started crying as I spoke. She told me everything would be ok and that we can handle this. I'll never forget that confidence and immediate support.

As the news spread about Luca's diagnosis, we were overwhelmed by the love and support that came our way. Our families, close friends, coworkers, friends we hadn't spoken to in years, and friends who were already part of the special needs community all reached out to share their love. I was welcomed into a Facebook group of moms who have kids with Down syndrome born in 2012 or 2013. It was an incredible comfort to be able to connect with moms with children around Luca's age, who were in the same stages of processing as I was. I learned quickly that this was going to be a place I could share some of my deepest, darkest, and brightest thoughts without judgment. That group was, and is, a lifeline to me.

In the beginning, I was fixated on the potential medical issues children with Ds may develop. Since the birth diagnosis was such a surprise after a rocky pregnancy, I had this creepy feeling of constantly waiting for the other shoe to drop. I read about everything from reflux to leukemia. There was so much to learn and be aware of and I did not want to miss a single cue.

It took me a solid three months to process Luca's Ds diagnosis. In those months, life felt like a rollercoaster. Not only were we grappling with what Ds would mean for Luca and our family, but we were trying to adjust to life with two children, in the midst of sleep deprivation. That was a tough few months!

For the next 2 months, we sorted out some early medical issues. Everything was very benign- Luca had reflux, laryngomalacia (floppy airway) and plagiocephaly which earned him a cool "space" helmet. I learned quickly what being my son's advocate meant as I had diagnosed each of these ailments and pushed my concerns forward to the doctors. I felt good that I was doing right by my son.

For the next 3 months, we enjoyed our son!!! Yes, it was finally at 5 months of age that we were starting to hit our stride! We had been working with a wonderful Early Intervention team for 2 months, and we were starting to think about his 6 month goals. That was when some worry started to creep back in.

Luca had been developing very close to the typical milestone timeline. Our goal had been to try to keep him as close to the typical timeframe as possible. At 6 months he was sitting up, rolling over from front-to-back and back-to-front, working on supporting himself on all fours, babbling, smiling and laughing all the time. But it seemed like he was starting to plateau. He started putting his hands in his mouth quite a bit, which prompted us all to suspect he was teething. I thought this seemed a little odd as I had read that kids with Ds may teethe late. And my daughter did not break her first tooth until she was 9 months old. I figured he was starting to feel those teeth early, and this would be a long teething process We started to have to move therapy session times around to try to catch him when he was more awake and not as bothered by his teeth.

Teething aside, we were about to go on vacation with some friends, and looking forward to introducing them to Luca. We were excited to get away as a family to do something "normal" and enjoy the beach together! Luca was so unusually cranky, I wanted to be certain he wasn't developing an ear infection, and took him in for one last check-up. The pediatrician cleared him and said there was no reason not to go on vacation!

Three days into the vacation, our world changed once again. Only we didn't know then quite how significantly. Luca started demonstrating an odd movement. He would throw his arms up and roll his eyes back. It was all very quick, like a startle. My stomach was in knots. I had watched videos about Infantile Spasms in those first few months because I wanted to know what to look for if Luca developed them. By the end of the trip, Luca was experiencing clusters of spasms. I was on the phone with his pediatrician while we were at the airport returning home begging for an appointment for the next day. Our flight home was diverted to the airport in Milwaukee, which was where Luca's specialists were, so I got off the plane with a medical emergency and brought him to the Emergency Room.

My mom and aunt met me in the ER and we worried deeply about what we were going to learn. The team there was very nice and explained that we had nothing to worry about. I showed them a video of the movements and Luca also did a few himself in the moment, and they assured us that these movements were not indicative of anything harmful for Luca. They sent us home with direction to have our pediatrician order an MRI and EEG for Luca. They couldn't do it themselves due to some insurance restrictions. I felt much better that we were given such a positive discharge.

The next day, the pit in my stomach returned as the frequency of the clusters increased. I fought hard to get in to see a pediatrician the next day, and finally, at 5pm when she saw the video and Luca demonstrate a spasm in the office, she was on the phone with the Children's hospital getting us admitted for a potential Infantile Spasms diagnosis.

On June 27, 2013, at nearly 9 months of age, Luca was diagnosed with Infantile Spasms (IS), a catastrophic seizure disorder. Hallmark symptoms of IS are developmental delays, regression, and mental retardation. Within a week of the diagnosis, we saw Luca lose nearly all of his milestones. We saw our son go from a smiling, laughing baby to a silent toddler who couldn't hold his head up. Loosing Luca's laughs and smiles hurt us the most.

Typically, children with Ds respond quickly to IS treatment, and are less likely to relapse. We faced his diagnosis with tenacity and convinced ourselves this would be a blip on our medical radar. Luca, however, took his own path once again, as he broke through 4 medications and developed 2 other seizure types. He spent time in the hospital every month for the next 6 months, was ambulanced twice, went through testing for metabolic disorders and mitochondrial disorders, and developed pneumonia which earned him a feeding tube. We longed for the days when he just had DS.

A few weeks after his first birthday, Luca smiled again. We had initiated the ketogenic diet and adjusted his medications and were cautiously optimistic that he was gaining seizure control. October 24, 2013 was the last time we saw Luca experience a seizure.

I have learned through his first year of life that the Ds diagnosis is a slippery slope. I spent 3 months processing, which I certainly needed, but now wish I had spent just truly enjoying my baby. I lived my life waiting for the other shoe to drop, rather than enjoying the moment. I realized that the developmental delays and cognitive impairment associated with Ds are just not a big deal to me.

When I worry about what the future will hold for Luca and our family, I realize it isn't a Ds diagnosis or an IS diagnosis that send me spinning. It's being a parent who is head over heels in love with her son and family and only wanting the best for them. I'm thankful to have my son, no matter what path his chromosomes send us down.

With all of the worry, fear, concern, sadness, and stress that has come with Luca's medical issues, I have to share that there has been incredible joy, love, support, selflessness, generosity and kindness brought into our lives. Our families will drop anything to help us out, our friends started a campaign to raise funds for Luca's care, my Facebook moms have sent cards and gifts with touching sentiments only they can share, a former colleague and her friends ran a marathon in his honor, and I've heard from old friends who found themselves down this special needs path offering me their support and shoulder to lean on if I need it.

At the end of the day, I focus less on the superficial and more on the real now. I've learned to truly take life one moment at a time. I'm curious to see what the future holds, but I stay in the now. And I never underestimate the healing powers of a pumpkin beer and hot shower.

{Nick, Gianluca's Dad}

"How are you doing with all of this?"

That's the signal that a conversation about Trisomy 21 is starting, and it means I better change my mood and get ready for a down and dirty honest conversation about our son, Gianluca.

My wife, Jenny, usually utters the above sentence while waving her hand around like Obi-Wan Kenobi trying to Jedi-mind-trick me into switching topics in our conversation.

It usually works, but not without some resistance on my part. I am certainly not some mindless storm trooper, but eventually the façade has to crack because that's how a marriage works, and it's especially true when dealing with a child like Gianluca.

Before that, though, Jenny has to force her way through my canned responses of "I'm OK. You?" I choose to deflect the question and give a standard response that harkens back to my days as a PR guy. Jenny usually continues to push it, and I give her a real answer because she's my wife and deserves the truth, and one of the reasons I married her is because she WILL push me and not settle on something that sounds like it came from a press release.

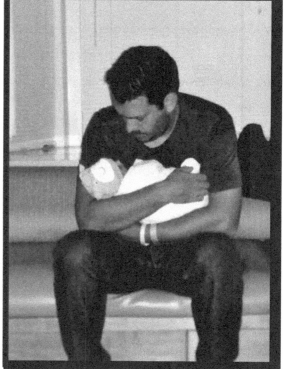

Trust me, I have a mental database of safe answers that would sound much more fitting coming out of a coach at a press conference or a politician trying to tip-toe around a potential controversy.

Then there's the reality, and that's exactly what Jenny wants. As my wife, she deserves it ... and so does Gianluca.

So, how am I doing? It depends on the day; some are good and some aren't. However, Gianluca's smile and gut-busting laugh makes it all fantastic, helmet and all.

When I think back to what it was like learning that our second – and most likely last – child was born with Trisomy 21, I just remember how misinformed we were. We had no idea what we were getting into, and no life experience with it. We found out after birth, and it hit us hard.

We knew there would be challenges, and we knew we would be up to face them together. One thing about us; we're strong and even stronger together.

Still, it was a rollercoaster of emotions, but only if the coaster went crashing to the ground as expectations and dreams were met with uncertainty and confusion.

We knew nothing. We just knew he would be different, and the emotions I felt were some of the rawest since experiencing the death of my Dad due to cancer in June 2000. You don't forget that feeling, which was brought back several years ago after Uncle Tommy's passing.

This time, we were starting not ending, and there were a lot of questions.

We have loving family and friends who showed tremendous support from around the world. It was truly overwhelming to get calls, emails, texts and whatever other correspondences sent to us. We knew we weren't alone in this. That's something we cherish, and will never forget, and it helped drive us.

Throughout our hospital stay, I was frequently in touch with my cousin Mary Jo, who is a doctor at Mount Sinai in New York. She would go on explaining to me what Down Syndrome was, and how Gianluca was going to be great and we were going to do everything we could to make sure of that.

Mary Jo's defiance to my ignorance included a telephone call with my sister Marcella and brother Giuseppe. Marcella is a middle school Italian teacher, and she was telling me about her experience with students who had Trisomy 21.

"They can learn a foreign language?!?!?" Yeah, I was that clueless.

After Mary Jo and Marcella set me straight, the switch was flipped.

Jenny and I would have long, difficult conversations throughout our hospital stay. There were tears, hugs, kisses, anger, sadness and finally smiles.

For all the raw emotion, I was able to draw the line; "We're still his parents. We have to do everything we can to help him."

You want to know how I'm doing? That's it right there. Every day that goes by, I just look at him as my amazing son. One day, I started to wonder what life would be like if he didn't have Down Syndrome. I stared at him, he looked at me, smiled and burst out with his laugh. I just said to him, "You wouldn't be Gianluca, and I WANT Gianluca."

He's our son and I can't imagine life without him, extra chromosome and all. Just like I can't imagine being without Jenny and our daughter Gabriella, whose unique personality keeps us on our toes and brightens up the room.

I would do anything for all of them, and I do.

Trisomy 21 may be something we have to overcome in some respects, but we'll do it together as a family, and that includes our extended family and friends. It may have surprised us, as life threw us a curveball, but we'll persevere and he'll be even better for it.

We can sit around blaming things; whatever deity you prefer, the doctors, each other, the randomness of the extra chromosome. You can waste your time and energy focusing on things that don't matter because you want answers or to place blame. That's wasted energy that should be focused on him, and the family. I don't have time for self-pity, and I don't have time to worry about what brought us here. We're here, so look forward to the challenges that we need to overcome.

That determination drives me. However, I don't want to think about the future when nothing is written. When I do, I make sure to pull myself back to reality and stay focused on the little guy.

Fantasy is for baseball and football, not raising kids.

We can influence this and help him achieve his potential, and we do that on a daily basis because he's our son, and we love him very much. I wouldn't want it any other way,

I'm doing great, and there's no need for tricks.

Thank you for reading our stories. We believe that the connections to other families can make all the difference when receiving a new diagnosis. Whether you have a prenatal or birth diagnosis, we are here for you. Check out our book of prenatal or potential diagnosis stories:

Expecting the Unexpected ~ Stories of a Down syndrome prenatal or potential diagnosis

Please visit our websites and Facebook pages for additional resources and support:

{Unexpected} - http://www.missiont21.com/

Down Syndrome Diagnosis Network - http://www.dsdiagnosisnetwork.org/